Becoming

BIBLE-
friendly

"... a motivational tool to encourage the reading
of the Word of God."

Robert C. Strubhar

WINEPRESS WP PUBLISHING

ISBN 1-57921-102-X
Library of Congress Catalog Card Number: 98-60198

To Jesus Christ, Who loved me and gave Himself for me.

Contents

Acknowledgments

In a very real sense, the producing of *Becoming Bible-Friendly* has been a family project. I am indebted to my beloved wife Verna of sixty-one years, who, with patience and perseverance, typed the entire manuscript with the exception of the foreword in its initial draft. With meticulous, untiring effort, she also served as proofreader. Her diligence and devotion to duty are highly prized and gratefully acknowledged, especially since she labored with physical limitations of almost total deafness and loss of body height of nearly eight inches caused by osteoporosis.

My oldest son, John, played a vital role in the production of the book, suggesting the title, reviewing the material with insightful editorial comments, and writing the foreword. Son Peter and daughter Mary were very supportive of me in this project. My son-in-law, G'Quintyn, provided additional computer support.

Pam Barcalow, wife of a former teaching colleague at Summit Christian College (now Taylor University Fort Wayne), retyped the completed first draft with characteristic expertise. Her attention to detail is self-evident.

I would be remiss indeed if I did not acknowledge the goodness of the Lord for His grace and help. There were many times when I reached an impasse in writing. I did not know what further word to communicate, but in His time and way, He scattered the clouds and shattered the obstacles, enabling me to finish what He put on my heart to do. To Him be eternal praise!

R.C.S.

Foreword

*B*ecoming *Bible-Friendly* is the life work of my father, who has devoted more than sixty years of his life to teaching and preaching the Word of God. Now in his eighties, he offers this book as the culmination of many hours spent alone in the presence of his closest friend, the Lord Jesus Christ!

From my earliest recollection, Dad has always had a passion for the Book. To paraphrase Charles Spurgeon, his blood is "bibline." From the time I was a youngster, I saw Dad on his knees in the early morning hours, studying the Scriptures and communicating with his heavenly Father. His "quiet time" discipline empowered him to be an effective transgenerational communicator and a relevant Bible teacher.

Recently George Gallup concluded that America is "a nation of biblical illiterates" (*US News & World Report*, April 4, 1995, 56–57). In other words, though many Americans believe the Bible, they do not read it or obey it. *Becoming Bible-Friendly* is aimed at correcting this national deficiency. Through a series of scriptural snapshots, the author introduces us to each of the sixty-six books of the Bible. Each section is a brief scriptural vignette, generally introduced, briefly outlined, and sprinkled with personal stories, illustrative lessons, and searching questions to whet our appetites for a daily diet of God's truth. By no means exhaustive, *Becoming Bible-Friendly* is an attempt to arrest the attention and interest of those who have lost their desire for Scripture reading and need a "jump start" to get going again.

My prayer is that this book will be a catalyst in bringing many "up to speed" in their understanding of God's purposes for their lives. *Becoming Bible-Friendly* is the only way to go!

JOHN R. STRUBHAR

Preface

A friend of yours is waiting in the wings. He has been there for ages, silent and perhaps neglected. Once in awhile you may give him a casual glance or consult him in times of trouble, but, for the most part, you have had little interest in him. Distancing yourself from him, you have missed his wise counsel and gentle nudges.

Do you know that your silent friend has a name? It is the Word of God, the Bible. He longs to take you by the hand and walk with you in your journey through life. He is a friend who sticks closer than a brother. He neither leaves you nor forsakes you. You can always depend on him, for he is true and faithful.

He is easy to become acquainted with, always available at any hour of the day or night. It is not possible for him to come to you, but you can always go to him. All he wants is your trust and openness. He has many things to say to you.

With the receiving of his message, significant spiritual experiences become yours—some of unspeakable joy and blessed assurance, others of deep heart-searching, calling for a confession of sin. At times you are given a sense of God's awesome presence, leading you to praise and worship. During troubles and tears, his comfort is incredible. His variety of ministries is never boring but always blessed.

What is your personal relationship to this wonderful friend? Is it a meaningful one, a casual one, a superficial one, a legalistic one, or an inconsistent one? Whatever it may be, let us begin where you are and work on nurturing a strong relationship with the Word of God.

This is the need of the hour. All too often Christians have neglected the Bible. Cal Thomas, quoting from the Gallup Poll, says: "Only eleven percent of people who claim to be believers read their Bible every day. That's your problem. If you are ignorant of the Word of God, you are going to be blind to the way of God and disobedient to the will of God" (*Christianity Today*, April 25, 1994).

This should change! The purpose of *Becoming Bible-Friendly* is to motivate individuals to get into the Word of God and allow the Word to get into them. Although there are many great books on the market—"how-to" books, family-life books, technical books, etc.—there is only one Book of books, the Bible. It deserves a hearing.

Accordingly, *Becoming Bible-Friendly* seeks to call attention to the value and importance of the Word of God with a minisurvey of all sixty-six books, structured around the following uniform methodology:

First, a brief *introduction* to each book in simple, understandable language is presented to arouse your interest and intensify your passion to read it regularly and thoughtfully.

Second, the *informational material* contains background facts to assist you in your understanding of the sixty-six books of the Bible.

Third, the *analytical overview* is a basic outline revealing the content of each biblical book. Studying the overview carefully as you read the text will enable you to interpret the message of the book accurately.

Fourth, the *practical aspects* amplify and illustrate how the truths of the book may be applied to your own life. Keep this important principle in mind as you read: There is *one* interpretation but *many* applications.

Preceding the minisurveys are two orientation chapters that deal with the *why* and *how* of *Becoming Bible-Friendly*.

To be a friend of the Bible is both challenging and rewarding. This blessed friendship made possible through the redeeming grace of God and the work of Jesus Christ yields rich dividends both now and forever. Your inner life and outward conduct will never remain on a mundane level but will be renewed and refreshed through a daily reading of the Bible and the teaching ministry of the Holy Spirit.

Blessings on you as you become Bible-friendly.

R.C.S.

Why Become Bible Friendly?

Early in life I felt my need for the Bible. I was five years old when my parents moved from a farm near Washington, Illinois, to a city, Peoria. The noises of this place were quite a contrast to the quiet of the country. The first time I heard the wail of the fire engines' sirens nearby I panicked, crying out, "Read the Bible to me. Read the Bible to me."

I was desperate, fearful, wondering what was going to happen to me. I needed the Bible when I was overwhelmed with fright. I wanted its words of assurance to quiet my anxious fears.

Personally I cannot imagine myself without the Bible. I would feel totally inadequate, apprehensive, and with a sense of great loss. It has been my constant companion for many years. I would never be without it.

This wonderful Book of books is unique. There is no other book in the world like it. It comes to us from God Himself, who moved upon the hearts and minds of his servants to give us his message. Therefore it deserves our deepest respect and highest praise.

The Enduring Word

The Psalmist declares, "Forever, O Lord, Thy word is settled in heaven" (Ps. 119:89 NASB). Someone has rightly commented, "It is settled there where the critics cannot get at it." Jesus reinforces this statement by saying, "Heaven and earth will pass away, but My words shall not pass away" (Matt. 24:35 NASB).

God's Word will outlast the present created order—that which is physical and material—because He is going to make a new heaven and a new earth (cf. Heb. 1:10–12; Rev. 21:1). The point is that wherever God is, whether in the present heaven or in the future heaven, His Word will forever be true. It cannot be destroyed.

The Bible has been given the most brutal and savage treatment possible, yet it continues to survive every vicious onslaught. The following poem by Clarence E. Flynn expresses it so well:

> They burned Truth in the marketplace
> And thought their work complete;
> But next day, with a smiling face,
> They met it on the street.
> They threw it in a dungeon damp
> And thought it was no more;
> But lo, it walked with lighted lamp
> Among them as before.
> They scorned and ostracized it
> And ordered it to depart;
> But still it dwelt in all the land
> And challenged every heart.[1]

The Bible cannot be conquered. It rides out every storm and outlives every critic. Men had better try to knock over the Empire State Building with a feather, bridge the ocean with a toothpick, dig the Panama Canal with a teaspoon, or melt the North Pole with a curling iron than attempt to destroy the Word of God. It is indestructible.

Therefore we can trust it always. It never leads us astray. It points out the right way in which to go. Genesis, the first book of the Bible, tells us from whence we have come; Revelation, the last book, where we are going. The Bible tells us how to live and how to die. It answers our questions and solves our problems. It is the divine absolute in this day of relativism.

THE ENLIGHTENING WORD

Again the Psalmist declares, "The entrance of your words gives light; it gives understanding to the simple" (Ps. 119:130 NIV). The Bible illuminates our thinking, providing us with correct information and godly instruction. Reading it makes us spiritually intelligent, keeping us updated in our ongoing walk with God. His Word molds our character, conforming us to the likeness of the "divine image."

Being enlightened by the Scriptures alerts us to dangers, soothes our fears, and arouses our emotions. God's Word picks us up when we are down, spurs us on when we are tempted to give up, and strengthens us in our weakness.

The Bible is pure light: "The words of the Lord are pure words; as silver tried in a furnace on the earth, refined seven times" (Ps. 12:6 NASB). It elevates our thinking from the garbage of vice and impurity. This is God's means of powerful protection from society's evil ills. Low morals taint and infect us. Unbridled liberties destroy us as unethical conduct pollutes us.

We have hit bottom morally. We need a lift to higher ground, a breath of fresh air in God's pure light.

The Enabling Word

That lift is found in the Bible. God's Word is innate with the power of the Spirit. Through this abundant provision, our sagging spirits can be strengthened; our dull minds sharpened; and our tired hearts quickened. The Word of God is powerful. It enables us to be growing Christians, developing in character and service. It comforts us, convicts us, cleanses us, and challenges us. It does wonders for us—without number!

The Bible is the book we need to get next to, to learn from, and to trust in. We need to make it our friend because it is always ready to be ours. Without this powerful Word to help us, we would be at a standstill, empty, negative, frustrated, sad, and lonely; but with it we are strengthened, encouraged, confident, satisfied, and fulfilled with the joy of the Lord.

Zwingli, one of the great reformers, explains:

> "We should hold the Word of God in the highest possible esteem—meaning by the Word of God only that which comes from the Spirit of God—and we should give to it a trust which we cannot give to any other word. For the Word of God is certain and can never fail. It is clear and will never leave us in darkness. It teaches its own truth. It arises and irradiates the soul of man with full salvation and grace. It gives the soul sure comfort in God."[2]

Do we not have reasons enough to become Bible-friendly?

How To Become Bible-Friendly?

To become Bible-friendly is not difficult. In fact, it is quite easy. All it takes is a ready mind and a willing heart to resolve purposefully to take up our Bible daily and read from its sacred pages. In so doing, we will joyfully discover that the longer we continue this practice, the sweeter it becomes.

Ultimately we will reach the point where we cannot do without it. This is good. Jesus Himself tells us: "Man shall not live on bread alone, but on every word that proceeds out of the mouth of God" (Matt. 4:4 NASB).

Becoming Bible-Friendly seeks to facilitate the precious process of digging into the Word of God on a daily basis. Therefore it is written in simple, understandable language, devoid of technical expressions and scholarly minutia.

This book is not designed to serve as a substitute for *Special Introduction,* which deals with issues such as authorship, canonicity, literary form, historical background, addressees, critical questions, characteristics, etc., of individual biblical books.

Actually, *Becoming Bible-Friendly* is a minisurvey of all the books comprising Scripture. There is a variety of subject matter to be found in each minisurvey, which may consist of personal incidents, practical applications, items of interest, and a comprehensive outline, serving as an overview of each book. The minisurvey is a concise introduction to the book selected by the reader and is designed to arouse his interest and whet his appetite for the Word of God.

Becoming Bible-Friendly is written for those who have a deep desire for accuracy, simplicity, challenge, forthrightness, and practical truths that may be applied to our lives everyday. Philosophical speculation is not given a place in these studies.

The Negative Approach

That being said, let me offer several suggestions leading to Bible friendliness. First, we should not approach Scripture with a negative attitude such as: "There is nothing in the Bible for me"; "It is too difficult to understand"; or "Why read it?" Such attitudes deprive us of the blessing of Bible reading. This inspired library of sixty-six books is a gift of God. Accept it thankfully.

Do not read the Bible *haphazardly,* such as looking at small portions of it once in a great while. This kind of reading does not give us a true picture of what Scripture actually teaches.

Do not read *selectively*—only that which appeals to personal interests and desires. Ultimately this may lead to imbalance, distortion, and even error. This is not to suggest that a study of various topics should not be pursued. Such studies are indeed profitable, if the verses considered are interpreted in light of their context.

Do not read *spasmodically,* consulting the Bible only on a hit-or-miss basis, according to one's feelings, whether high or low, allowing the degree of emotion to determine the decision to read or not to read.

Do not read *quantitatively,* seeking to cover a certain amount of chapters at one sitting. Reading with haste and without thinking blurs meaning. Covering great amounts of material does not make for fulfillment or significance.

THE POSITIVE APPROACH

Aim at *quality* reading, which means coming to the Bible with an open mind, recognizing it as the "Supreme Court of Authority," and worthy of your confident trust. It is always the "thus says the Lord," which is the determining factor in all matters of faith and practice. Every thought and preconceived notion is to submit to what the Bible says. Read *submissively.*

Read *prayerfully,* asking the Lord to open His Word to you. He is pleased when we acknowledge Him. He responds to us. In fact, He has already made provision in the Holy Spirit to guide us into all truth (John 16:13).

Read *devotedly,* resolving to give quality time in your day for this important spiritual exercise. Moreover, determine to finish the reading of one book before going on to another.

Read *preparedly*—with a pen in hand and a notebook by your side in order to record the thoughts that come to your mind. At first there may be little to record, but keep on with the practice of writing regardless. In time, gems of recorded thoughts will become rich dividends.

Read *obediently*. Walk in the light of eternal truth, blending your whole being with it, absorbing it like a sponge. This discipline molds you into a vessel useful for the Master (2 Tim. 2:21). Moreover, it has a cleansing effect in your life (John 15:3).

Read *expectantly*. God intends to bless you through His Word. As He opens it up, your joy increases and you will exclaim, "I see something in the Scriptures that I have not been aware of before. This is exciting. How wonderful is His Word."

Freely use *Becoming Bible-Friendly*. Refer frequently to the table of contents. It will assist you in choosing a book of the Bible to read. After making your selection, turn to the minisurvey for an overview and practical application. Then go to the Bible and read, think, and study. Because we live in New Testament times, it is suggested that those books be read first. However, Old Testament books should not be neglected nor considered less important. The ideal way is to combine both in your reading.

My prayer is that *Becoming Bible-Friendly* will ignite your heart with a new passion for God's Book!

THE OLD TESTAMENT BOOKS

"When your words came, I ate them; they were my joy and my heart's delight." (Jer. 15:16a, NIV)

Genesis: Value Your Roots

Do you ever wonder where you came from? Have these questions puzzled you: Who am I? Why am I here? Where am I going? The first book of the Bible, Genesis, gives us some simple, correct answers.

Genesis provides the deep roots for Christianity. It is a basic book revealing origins, namely, of the created world, mankind, nations, and the redemptive process whereby God raises up for Himself a people of faith and obedience.

The vital historical facts given in this book provide a firm foundation for our faith. Authentic biblical faith is based on historical truth, not on philosophical or theoretical concepts. Genesis furnishes evidence that Christianity is not simply a theory but an actuality, because a redeemed man is brought into a personal relationship with God. It can be truthfully said, "This actually happened in history." Therefore ours is a valid faith. It has historical roots. Value your roots.

INFORMATIONAL MATERIAL

The title, Genesis, according to the Hebrew text, means "in the beginning." The Greek word means "origin" or "beginning." This book, written by Moses, is the first book of the Pentateuch. It is an account of beginnings. "These are the generations" (2:4; 5:1; 6:9; 10:1; 11:10, 27; 25:12, 19; 37:2 KJV). "This is the account" (NASB).

Genesis contains foundational truths of various disciplines. G. Campbell Morgan spells them out as follows (an adaption):

Theology (truth about God). God is presented as Creator, Sovereign, Redeemer, Mighty One, Shepherd, Rock of Israel, and the Almighty.

Cosmology (the origin, structure, and space-time relationships of the universe). 'The whole universe has come into being by the will and act of God. The hallmark of the Divine handiwork is upon every blade of grass and every flaming constellation.'

Anthropology (study of man). 'Man is a mingling of dust and Deity by the will and act of God; a being placed under authority, and having dominion over all things beneath him: a being responsible, therefore, to God.'

Sociology (study of human relationships, study of society, social institutions, and social relationships). The vital unit of a family is based on a marriage relationship. A nation is comprised of families who are ultimately responsible to God.

Ethnology (deals with the division of mankind into races). The godlessness of the human race fractured its unity. The account of the Tower of Babel gives historical evidence of this fact.

Hamartiology (doctrine of sin). Sin is disobedience, transgression, and rebellion against God. The judgment of God upon sin is death.

Soteriology (doctrine of salvation). God Himself is the author of salvation. Man's only hope is found in the Redeemer—the God of Abraham, Isaac, and Jacob.[3]

ANALYTICAL OVERVIEW

I. Creation (1:1–2:25)
   A. Of the world (1:1–2:3)
   B. Of mankind (2:4–25)
II. Degeneration (3:1–11:32)
   A. The Fall (3:1–5:32)
   B. The flood (6:1–10:32)
   C. The failure (11:1–32)
III. Transformation (12:1–50:26)
   A. Abraham (12:1–25:11)
   B. Isaac (25:12–28:9)
   C. Jacob (Joseph) (28:10–50:26)

PRACTICAL ASPECTS

In these changing times, there are some things that never change: male and female, family, moral values such as purity, virginity, honesty, integrity, and virtue. These values—ordained by God and deeply rooted in history—are for the good of mankind. Today the nuclear family is being sacrificed on the altar of infidelity. Genesis teaches us that family life goes back to the very beginning of the human race. It serves as a cornerstone of society.

Genesis is quoted and referred to many times in the New Testament. Jesus Himself draws from this authentic source of truth as He teaches on the subject of marriage (Mark 10:6–9). Paul refers to Genesis in telling about the Fall (1 Tim. 2:13–14). Peter writes about Abraham and Sarah in regard to the marriage relationship (1 Pet. 3:4–7). James calls Abraham the friend of God (James 2:23). The writer of Hebrews acknowledges many of the individuals mentioned in Genesis: Abel, Enoch, Noah, Abraham, Sarah, Isaac, Jacob, Esau, and Joseph (11:4–22). Jude tells of "Enoch, in the seventh generation from Adam" (Jude 14). John uses Cain as an example not to follow (1 John 3:12). Revelation refers to Jesus as the "Lion from the tribe of Judah" (Rev. 5:5). All of these statements establish the historicity of Genesis.

This book points out man's weaknesses, sins, and failures. The authentic account given does not gloss over the sordid record of his depravity. God hates sin and punishes it. Nevertheless, He loves the sinner and makes provision to forgive him. The God revealed in Genesis is also a God of grace and goodness.

Before man was ever brought on the scene, Genesis tells us of God's activity. He makes the material universe: light, sky, land, vegetation, sun, moon, stars, fish, birds, land animals, and finally, man. God first prepares a place for man, after which He creates him. God prepared this magnificent universe for mankind, so think of what He is preparing for His redeemed people now. Significantly Jesus says, "I go to prepare a place for you" (John 14:2). What a place this will be!

Exodus: Celebrate Your Deliverance

Exodus is the Mosaic account of the divine process in taking a people from their forefathers—Abraham, Isaac, and Jacob—and making out of them a nation to show forth His excellencies. The mighty God delivers Israel from Egyptian bondage, sustains them in the wilderness, and enters into a covenant relationship with them. Moreover, He gives them the Ten Commandments and various laws, statutes, and ordinances, along with specific directions to construct a tabernacle for Himself that He "may dwell among them" (25:8).

The Lord raises up this entire nation in order that it might be a kingdom of priests and a holy people, "His treasured possession" (19:5–6). These are a special people of faith, who are to express themselves to God in worship and obedience.

INFORMATIONAL MATERIAL

The Hebrews call this second book of the Bible, "And these are the names of." The Septuagint title means "exit," "departure," "a going out."

Exodus ties in with Genesis concerning God's revelation of Himself. He is the God of Abraham, the God of Isaac, and the God of Jacob (Gen. 28:13; Exod. 3:6). Exodus confirms the promise of God to give the land to Israel (Gen. 15:18; Exod. 13:5). Joseph is so confident that Israel would depart from Egypt that he makes his people promise to carry his bones with them (Gen. 50:25; Exod. 13:19). Furthermore, the time element of Israel's sojourn in Egypt is mentioned in both books (Gen. 15:13; Exod. 12:40–41).

This book opens on a sad note: God's people, so abundantly blessed through Abraham, Isaac, Jacob, and Joseph, and honored by Pharaoh, are now oppressed. A new Egyptian king stands vehemently against them. Israel is enslaved by cruel taskmasters (1:11). Their male population is threatened, yet they continue to multiply. In these depressing circumstances, God does not forget His people. To confirm this, He rescues them. The day is not too far off when Israel's sighs will be turned into songs (Exod. 15).

> Exodus is a revelation of the procedure of God in human history. . . . It is the story of the nation . . . who under His government should reveal in the world the breadth and beauty and beneficence of that government; a people who, gathered in their national life about His throne and His altar, obeying His commands and worshiping Him, shall reveal to outside nations the meaning of the Kingship of God.[4]

The book closes on an upbeat note: "The glory of the Lord filled the tabernacle" (40:34–35). The slaves of Egypt, now free, are the servants of God Who is dwelling among them.

ANALYTICAL OVERVIEW

I. The deliverance from Egypt (1:1–15:21)
    A. Moses the deliverer (1:1–7:7)
    B. The ten plagues upon Egypt (7:8–12:36)
    C. The beginning of the journey (12:37–15:21)
II. The journey in the wilderness (15:22–18:27)
    A. God performs miracles (15:22–17:16)
    B. Jethro counsels Moses (18:1–27)
III. The revelation at Mount Sinai (19:1–34:35)
    A. The giving of the law and ordinances (19:1–24:18)
    B. The plan for the tabernacle (25:1–34:35)
IV. The response of the people (35:1–40:38)
    A. Their work accomplished (35:1–39:43)
    B. Their worship established (40:1–38)

PRACTICAL ASPECTS

Liberated people require an authority over them, or they will lapse into complacency. They always need the Lord and His Word; otherwise, their liberty-loving natures will lead them to carelessness. A moral consciousness needs to be established within them to give an awareness of right and wrong; therefore, God gives them the Law to guide them and protect them. He does not want His people, who are free indeed, going astray.

Common events play a vital role in the life of Moses (e.g., the common practice of bathing paves the way for Pharaoh's daughter to go to the river and discover Moses in a basket among the reeds [2:1–10]; a common act of kindness, watering a flock of sheep [2:17], opens the door to hospitality and marriage; faithfulness in life's daily routines— simply doing what is supposed to be done, performing mundane tasks—leads to the burning bush experience [3:1–4:16]). God often uses ordinary events and common practices in life to open doors of opportunity. Our Lord is in more of the commonplace events than we think He is. Insignificant happenings turn out to be highly significant.

The God who reveals Himself to men in Genesis is the same God who speaks to Moses (3:15). The Lord speaks and acts in every generation, remembering His promises. Moses does not discover this "Great God; the Strong One; the Self-existent, Eternal One." He is revealed to him, not as a new God, but the same One from the beginning. The God of the twentieth century is also the God of the Old Testament. The true believer today trusts the same eternal God and is in the same stream of history.

We who have been set free from bondage, like Israel, have a joyous song of triumph (15:1–18); therefore, let us celebrate our deliverance.

Leviticus: Authenticate Your Worship

L eviticus is a revelation of the holiness of God who demands a holy people. These special people are set apart to worship Him.

This third book of Moses meaning "pertaining to the Levites," is an inspired manual setting forth the essentials and requirements of true worship. Those of the tribe of Levi are chosen to serve as priests in the tabernacle; other Levites are given responsibilities of the care and transportation of the tabernacle.

If one is to be an authentic worshiper of the Lord, he is required to approach God in the manner ordained by Him. He is not permitted to come before the Lord according to his own plan or works. The Hebrews are not to develop their own patterns for worship.

Informational Material

This book comes to the people of God with divine authority. The verb "to speak" is used thirty-eight times. God speaks to Moses and Aaron. "No other book in the Bible affirms divine inspiration so frequently as Leviticus."[5] These commands are given to Moses on Mount Sinai.

The key thought of Leviticus is holiness. The word "holy" is mentioned more than eighty times. It means that which is devoted and dedicated, given wholly and purposely to the Lord, to be separated unto Him for His purposes. Basically, man is estranged from God because of his sin. In the Levitical system of worship, there is a recognition of the defilement of sin in light of the holiness of God. A provision is made for the forgiveness and cleansing of sin through the plenteous redemption springing from the love of God.

This handbook on worship gives us the "how-to" of drawing near to God for both priests and the people. Worship according to God's way is authentic devotion.

It has been said of Leviticus that it is "the most thoroughly legalistic of all the books of the Old Testament which more clearly sets forth the redemption which is in Christ."[6] Certainly, this is the evidence of the grace of God in the Old Testament dispensation.

Leviticus reveals the provision for worship, the requirements for worship, and the times for worship. In order to gain a better understanding of the book, it is suggested that the Book of Hebrews be read before and after a study of Leviticus.

ANALYTICAL OVERVIEW

I. The essentials of worship (1:1–10:20)
    A. The offerings of the people (1:1–6:7)
    B. The ministry of priests (6:8–10:20)
II. The directives for worshipers (11:1–27:34)

A. Dietary standards (11:1–47)
B. Childbirth purification (12:1–8)
C. Disease and discharge cleansing (13:1–15:33)
D. Day of Atonement ordinances (16:1–34)
E. Personal and social relationships (17:1–22:33)
F. Worship schedule (23:1–44)
G. Priestly responsibilities (24:1–23)
H. Significant years and laws (25:1–55)
I. Rewards and punishment (26:1–46)
J. Vows and dedications (27:1–34)

PRACTICAL ASPECTS

Certainly, there is need for a study of Leviticus today. This is not to suggest that we go back to the Old Testament forms of worship. We are living in New Testament times, and we recognize Jesus Christ as our supreme sacrifice. He gave Himself for us that we might be in a right relationship with a holy God and have fellowship with Him.

Leviticus contains timeless principles and values of which our generation needs to be aware, incorporating them into our worship, such as purity, humility, reverence, obedience, and sincerity.

God alone, not the form or method, is to be worshiped. He is holy, righteous, and just. He says, "Be holy, for I am holy" (11:45). A holy God demands and deserves a holy people. Another impressive truth springing out of Leviticus is this: Never take sin lightly; God doesn't. G. Campbell Morgan's terse statements say it well:

Sin is unlikeness to God. . . . Sin is distance from God. . . . Sin is wrong done to God. . . . Redemption is founded upon righteousness. . . . Redemption is only possible by blood. . . . Redemption is in order to holiness. . . . Redemption does not excuse a man from holiness. It is the method by which man is made holy.[7]

In Leviticus, the authentic worshiper looks beyond the sacrifice he is offering to God Himself. Significant expressions such as "to the Lord" (1:2; 2:1; 4:3), "before the Lord" (1:5; 3:1; 4:4), and "of the Lord" (1:2, 13; 22:22–27) are repeated again and again. This indicates that salvation is in a Person—God Himself—and not in a performance. These expressions create a God-awareness in the heart of the worshiper.

Dr. Warren Wiersbe's working definition of worship is noteworthy:

> Worship is the believer's response of all that he is—mind, emotions, will, and body—to all that God is and says and does. This response has its mystical side in subjective experience and its practical side in objective obedience to God's revealed truth. It is a loving response as the believer comes to know God better.[8]

Worship is an inward awareness, an emotion expressing itself in awe, wonder, and love to the magnificent God Who is truly our Father. It is a heart in touch with heaven in an indescribable closeness that causes us to cry out, "My Lord and my God, how great and glorious You are. I love You. I worship You. There is none like You. Glory to You, Father, Son, and Holy Spirit."

Numbers: Obey Your Orders

Numbers, the fourth book of the Pentateuch, bears a close relationship to Exodus and Leviticus (Exod. 40:34–35; Lev. 1:1; Num. 1:1), both in the time period covered and with regard to content.

The book reveals the activity of God in taking a liberated people from Egyptian bondage, and through instructional and disciplinary means, seeking to shape them into a unique nation. Nationally, at this point in time, Israel is in her infancy. She needs teaching, testing, and stretching in order to mature and to prepare for conquest in the Promised Land. She must learn to obey God because freedom is not an escape from rule.

INFORMATIONAL MATERIAL

To the Hebrews, the book is known by the phrase "in the wilderness," the fifth word of the book. The Septuagint translation calls it Numbers, probably because there is a "prominence of census figures." G. Campbell Morgan observes that there is a month between the story with which Exodus ends and that with which Numbers begins.[9] Between the beginning and the end of the book is a period of thirty-eight to forty years.

Numbers tells the sad story of disobedience to God, resulting in wandering and confusion. On the other hand, it shows the obedience of the leader Moses who carries out the commandments of God meticulously. "Moses did as the Lord commanded him" (27:22).

New Testament roots are found in Numbers. Jesus makes reference to the bronze serpent lifted up by Moses in the wilderness (21:9) in His dialogue with Nicodemus (John 3:14–15). Jude writes about the "error of Balaam" and the "rebellion of Korah" (Jude 11). Peter also tells of Balaam who "loved the ways of unrighteousness" (2 Pet. 2:15–16).

The Old Testament writers draw from truths found in Numbers, which the Holy Spirit prompted them to include in their writings (e.g., "The Lord make His face shine upon you" [Num. 6:25; see Ps. 80:3, 7, 19]; Jeremiah quotes from Numbers, "A fire has gone forth from Heshbon" [Jer. 48:45; Num. 21:28]; Hosea refers to the shameful acts of Israel at Baal-Peor [Num. 25:3; Hos. 9:10]).

The Book of Numbers is largely narrative in form, interspersed with numerous historical facts, instructional data, and a collection of statistics.

The priestly benediction, known and loved by true worshipers everywhere, is found in 6:24–26.

ANALYTICAL OVERVIEW

I. The encampment in Sinai (1:1–10:10)
   A. The people mobilized (1:1–4:49)
   B. Additional laws given (5:1–6:27)
   C. The tabernacle consecrated (7:1–10:10)
II. The journeys in the wilderness (10:11–21:35)
   A. The trials and triumphs (10:11–12:16)

PRACTICAL ASPECTS

Numbers shows the importance of obeying God at all costs. One of the grievous sins of Israel is disobedience. The tragic experience at Kadesh-Barnea; the rebellion of Korah, Dathan, and Abiram; and even the disobedience of Moses in the Desert of Zin prove that disobedience is devastating. How right and rewarding is obedience.

Although God is developing a nation, He never loses sight of the individual. The individual is vitally important to God. The evidence for this fact is found in the various lists of individual persons mentioned (1:5–15; 1:20–46; 2:1–32; 3:21–31; 7:12–83; 13:4–15; 34:19–29).

This book yields a strategy that the church of Jesus Christ can effectively use in today's world. Wisely, many have picked up on this, utilizing a number of these biblical concepts dealing with organization.

Unfortunately, others have neglected or bypassed organizational procedures, calling them unspiritual or too binding on their Christian liberties. They must go by "the Spirit," i.e., by impulse. They shun organization like the plague. They have been influenced by those who have suggested that organization is of the devil. Nothing is further from the truth. God has His universe—and the human body—highly organized.

The church also needs organization because it is Christ's body. A body organized can function properly and accomplish great things because it follows in the steps of Deity.

Moses serves as an outstanding model of a leader. In assigning tasks to the Levites, he gives clear-cut job descriptions. In studying these carefully, a church leader can gain excellent insights as to what is to be included in a job description.

Liberated people need divine orders. Numbers discloses many of them for those freed from Egyptian bondage. As God puts together a nation socially (1:52–2:34), militarily (1:20–46), and spiritually (1:50–51; 3:5–39), He seeks to make it strong by giving it commands and orders. True freedom is not an escape from the rule of divine authority; therefore, obey your orders.

Deuteronomy: Claim Your Inheritance

The title of this book means "second law" or "repetition of the law." Luther speaks of it as a summary of the whole law and wisdom of the people of Israel, which includes such things as they are generally required to know.

Deuteronomy comes to us from a Spirit-inspired man who knows the reality of a face-to-face relationship with God (34:10). "Its supreme and overwhelming message is that of love. . . . God's love of man is the motive of His government; and . . . man's love of God is the motive of his obedience."[10] Deuteronomy is a revelation of the exalted nature of God and the responsibility of His redeemed ones to reflect that nature.

This book gives us an awareness of the greatness of God. The evidence of that greatness is observed in the promises He keeps (1:10–11), the provisions He makes (1:21), the power He manifests (1:30–31), and the providence He exercises (1:38–39).

INFORMATIONAL MATERIAL

Moses is the author of Deuteronomy. The place of his writing is in the wilderness, an unlikely place, indeed, for ministry. Nevertheless, God speaks to him and to a multitude of people through him. From that barren country leaps the eternal Word that ultimately girdles the entire globe.

Bible scholars have observed that Deuteronomy is one of the most eloquent books of the Bible, forceful and persuasive. Yet its writer confesses, "I am not eloquent" (Exod. 4:10).

The thrust of the Mosaic message is preparation, getting God's people ready for the conquest of Canaan. How carefully and faithfully does Moses seek to lay the groundwork for this difficult mission in the enemies' domain. Israel engages in titanic battles, but with absolute dependence on their mighty God and obedience to His Word, they are victorious.

Three key expressions are used by Moses throughout the book many times: "the Lord your God," "possess," and "the land which the Lord God gives." This emphasis makes Israel aware of the divine resources they have at their disposal and of their responsibilities to obey God. Thus, they can claim their inheritance.

"The New Testament contains over eighty citations of and references to Deuteronomy: These must be studied if the meaning of the book is to be understood and its message received."[11]

Jesus Christ Himself quotes three verses from Deuteronomy to defeat Satan: "Man shall not live by bread alone" (Deut. 8:3; Matt. 4:4); "You shall not put the Lord your God to the test" (Deut. 6:16; Matt. 4:7); "You shall worship the Lord your God and serve Him only" (Deut. 6:13; Matt. 4:10).

ANALYTICAL OVERVIEW

I. Introduction (1:1–4)
   A. The writer (1:1*a*)
   B. The place and time of writing (1:1*b*–4)
II. The first discourse (1:5–4:43)
   A. The review of the past (1:5–3:29)
   B. The exhortation to obedience (4:1–43)
III. The second discourse (4:44–26:19)
   A. The revelation of God at Sinai (4:44–5:33)
   B. The commandments, statutes, and judgements (6:1–26:19)
IV. The third discourse (27:1–30:20)
   A. Directives for life in Canaan (27:1–10)
   B. The curses of disobedience (27:11–26)
   C. The blessings of obedience (28:1–14)
   D. Additional curses for disobedience (28:15–68)
   E. The covenant renewed (29:1–30:20)
V. Conclusion (31:1–34:12)
   A. Moses succeeded by Joshua (31:1–29)
   B. Moses' song (31:30–32:52)
   C. Moses' blessing (33:1–29)
   D. Moses' death (34:1–12)

PRACTICAL ASPECTS

In His dealings with Israel, God has an objective in mind. He brings His people out of Egypt with a mighty hand to lead them to the Promised Land. The divine process through which He works requires faith, obedience, and perseverance. At times there are testings, problems, difficulties, and even pain, but all of these realities bring the people closer

45

to their desired haven. Finally they enter Canaan. God does what He says He will do for His people.

Our Lord has plans for us. He takes us from the old life, gives us a brand-new life from the inside out in order to take us to be with Him in His time. The process from spiritual birth to eternal glory is planned by Him. Since He knows what He is doing, we can safely trust Him.

This reminds me of an experience in California when I learned about the process of turning stone into cement. First, the stone is blasted from the quarry. By the power of God, like dynamite, we are freed from the bondage of sin.

The stone is carried in trucks to a crusher, which looks like an ice cream freezer. From there it goes on conveyor belts to be mixed with other ingredients in great rolling drums with steel balls. It is ground to powder, then put in water and finally fire. It is subjected to beatings, grindings, water, and fire. When men and machines have conquered the stone, it becomes cement—useful for many things.

The Christian life is like this. God takes us as "raw products," saves us, matures us through His processes, and makes us useful on earth and in eternity.

Joshua: Overcome Your Adversaries

The Book of Joshua is a record of God's faithfulness to His people in fulfilling His promises to them (21:43–45; 23:14). No promise fails; each one comes to pass. After confronting and overcoming many powerful adversaries, Israel finally conquers the land and receives the inheritance, which is divided by lot among the tribes. The chosen people of God discover the Canaan land to be a battleground.

Initially, the Lord gives the promises to Abraham and confirms them to the following generations, ultimately fulfilling them many years later under the leadership of Joshua. This book tells us that God is true to His Word. He is trustworthy; His Word is reliable. Now at long last, Israel is in the Promised Land; thus, a new phase of living is introduced to these recipients of the promises.

INFORMATIONAL MATERIAL

The Book of Joshua is written by a man whose name means "salvation." It is also apparent by internal evidence that the Holy Spirit uses other men of God to assist in the writing, since one of the writers mentions the death of Joshua (24:29–31).

In the Hebrew Bible, Joshua is placed first in the second division called "the early prophets," which includes Joshua, Judges, Samuel, and Kings. The early prophets cover the period of Israel's history from the invasion of Canaan to the Exile. Some scholars suggest that the events described in the book occurred about 1400 B.C.

With the land now divided and allotted, Israel experiences social change. No longer are they a people in bondage, nor are they wanderers in the wilderness. Now they are at home. They have a land of their own as God promised them.

The Book of Joshua records some incredible, awe-inspiring miracles; e.g., the crossing of the Jordan River during flood stage (4:22–24), the collapsing of the walls of Jericho (6:20), and the extending of a day during which time "the sun stood still, and the moon stopped" (10:12–14).

In addition, this book is a "link between the death of Moses and the death of Joshua, and covers a period of forty-five to fifty years in the history of the ancient people."[12]

ANALYTICAL OVERVIEW

I. The invasion and conquest of Canaan (1:1–12:24)
   A. God's command to Joshua (1:1–9)
   B. Preparations for the invasion (1:10–2:24)
   C. The crossing of the Jordan (3:1–4:24)
   D. Circumcision at Gilgal (5:1–12)
   E. The fall of Jericho (5:13–6:27)
   F. The tragedy and triumph over Ai (7:1–8:35)
   G. The Gibeonite deception (9:1–27)

    H. The kings and cities conquered (10:1–12:24)
II. The division and allotment of Canaan (13:1–22:34)
    A. Division of the land east of the Jordan (13:1–33)
    B. Division of the land west of the Jordan (14:1–15)
    C. Allotment of the land for the tribes (15:1–19:51)
    D. Cities of refuge designated (20:1–9)
    E. Cities assigned to the Levites (21:1–45)
    F. Tribes east of the Jordan return home (22:1–34)
III. The final words of Joshua (23:1–24:33)
    A. The farewell message (23:1–16)
    B. The covenant renewed (24:1–33)

PRACTICAL ASPECTS

One of the important truths often overlooked in our times, which is very much in evidence in Joshua, is that God enlightens pagan people. He does it in Old Testament times; He is doing it today. Rahab, the prostitute, knows that the Lord is giving the land to Israel (2:9), that the Lord is drying up the "water of the Red Sea" (2:10), and that the Lord has defeated Sihon and Og (2:10). When she and others hear it, their hearts melt. She confesses, "The Lord your God, He is God in heaven above and on earth beneath" (2:11). This news causes Rahab to repent and to plead for mercy. The other inhabitants of Jericho hear the same news, but they do not believe nor repent. It is apparent that the majority of people do not act on the light they receive. They reject it. Therefore they cannot blame God for their darkness (Rom. 1).

Furthermore, the kings of the Amorites and the Canaanites hear how the Lord has dried up the Jordan (5:1). Pagan people are enlightened with truth. When light comes to them they fear, but they fight against God and His people Israel. Natural man hates light because his deeds are evil (John 3:19). Therefore, God cannot be charged with man's darkness. Man is in darkness because he wants to be. It is the nature of God to dispel darkness with light.

This book throbs with action. God's people are aggressive and on the offensive. They are going places and doing things. The Book of Joshua is comparable to the Book of Acts, which tells of the church on the move. God's people are never to be on the defensive or fight in a rearguard action.

Remember, life is a continuous battle. We never reach a place where the battles are over—only when we are dead. After one battle, we forge ahead to engage the enemy in a new battle. We camp against him. We regroup our forces, bring in fresh supplies, rethink our strategies, renew our strength, and continue trusting God. Then we fight against our enemies with fresh vigor. We capture them, overthrow them, and defeat them utterly. Once again we press on. We are out to take Canaan land. Overcome your adversaries.

God is not finished with older people, those over sixty-five. Joshua is probably in his late eighties or early nineties, and Caleb is eighty-five when the Lord is using them. God uses the old as well as the young.

The Lord acknowledges the reality of old age, and so must we. We cannot deny it; therefore, accept it (13:1). Even though there is no fountain of youth for a body that goes through the aging process, yet the inner man is being renewed day by day (2 Cor. 4:16).

In old age, God accommodates Himself to us. He gives us a different role. In his younger days, Joshua took an active part in combat on the battlefield. In his later years, his role was more administrative, delegating authority to others (18:4–7). God takes age into consideration as He leads us.

As a leader, Joshua serves as a shining example for excellent management: He has an objective in view; he knows what personnel to use; he delegates responsibility; he demands accountability; he recognizes the chain of authority; he gives clear explanations; he reaches his goals; he gives precise orders; he tells why certain things are to be done; he builds on the work of others; he does good things for others; he recognizes his accountability; and he is true to his word (18:4–10).

We need this book of encouragement. It firms up our spiritual muscles. We must guard against getting soft, lazy, and careless. We must live by the Word of God. It gives us balance (23:6–10).

Judges: Learn Your Lessons

This book is a record of life in the Israelite nation under the authority of an individual who is known as a judge. The primary sense of the Hebrew word, "judge," is that of exercising the processes of government in its judicial functions. The judge acts as a ruler (king) and decides cases of controversy in civil, domestic, and religious areas. Primarily, the judge is a military leader in battle and a ruler in peace (2:18). In dispensing justice, he punishes the evildoer and vindicates the righteous.

The Lord raises up judges after His people have grievously sinned and are delivered into the hands of their enemies (2:16). When sin is acknowledged, confessed, and repented of, the compassionate God brings help to the nation by giving them a judge who leads them in conquest over all their enemies. In the Promised Land a new order of administering justice now emerges after the death of Joshua.

INFORMATIONAL MATERIAL

Judges gives us the history of Israel from Joshua to Samuel. The time period covered in the book is approximately three hundred years, from 1370 to 1020 B.C.

The author is not named, and the date of the writing of the book cannot be precisely stated. Some scholars suggest that the human writer could have been Samuel or one of his followers. It is observed that the Hebrew text of Judges is the best preserved of all the books comprising the former prophets.

Payne says of the author that he is "one of civilization's first true historians, not simply recording events, but then interpreting the facts on the basis of an explicit philosophy of history."[13]

The book itself begins on a high note and ends on a low one. At the very first, God is acknowledged (1:1); at the end a statement gives insight as to how far Israel has fallen from her lofty height. "In those days Israel had no king; everyone did as he saw fit" (21:25 NIV). There it is—de-generation—going from God to self. That is one side of the tragic story of Judges: apathy leading to apostasy, and apostasy leading to God's anger and His righteous judgment. The other side is restoration. The compassionate God forgives His wayward people and restores them to His favor on the basis of repentance.

Reference is made to several of the judges in the Book of Hebrews (11:32), indicating that the New Testament writer is acquainted with the truths of this book. Named are Gideon, Barak, Samson, and Jephthah.

When reading Judges, remember that some of the stories are often cruel. "It should not be imagined that the writer is approving of everything which he records. Rather, the book should be viewed as a story of the tragic judgment of God upon a people who failed to keep their heritage of true religious faith by assimilating far too much of their surrounding culture."[14]

ANALYTICAL OVERVIEW

I. Events before the judgeship (1:1–2:9)
  A. Battles against the Canaanites (1:1–36)
  B. Visit of the angel (2:1–5)
  C. The death of Joshua (2:6–9)
II. Individuals given the judgeship (2:10–16:31)
  A. Othniel (2:10–3:11)
  B. Ehud (3:12–30)
  C. Shamgar (3:31)
  D. Deborah and Barak (4:1–5:31)
  E. Gideon (6:1–8:35)
  F. Abimelech (9:1–57)
      Note: Abimelech is considered an outlaw or usurper, rather than a judge.
  G. Tola (10:1–2)
  H. Jair (10:3–5)
  I. Jephthah (10:6–12:7)
  J. Ibzan (12:8–10)
  K. Elon (12:11–12)
  L. Abdon (12:13–15)
  M. Samson (13:1–16:31)
III. Life during the judgeship (17:1–21:25)
      Note: Many call this division an appendix.
  A. The compromising Levite (17:1–18:31)
  B. The degrading practices (19:1–30)
  C. The warring tribes (20:1–48)
  D. The grieving nation (21:1–25)

PRACTICAL ASPECTS

"Learn your lesson" is one of the practical exhortations that may be deduced from the teachings of this book. This is where the people of God, now in the Promised Land, fail miserably. They do not learn from history that a right relationship with God is an absolute necessity.

Israel is on a roller coaster, up and down in its relationship with their Lord. Consequently, the nation sins and suffers as it goes downward, but upon repentance and restoration, it moves upward. Up again, down again; off again, on again—the tragic results of doublemindedness, disobedience, doubt, and disbelief. When will Israel learn its lessons from history: Always maintain a right relationship with the Lord. We must never, never, never let our environment or culture pressure us to break a sacred bond with God. The speed with which we forget our lessons so easily is incredible.

A careful study of chapter one discloses what leads to degeneration, disaster, and defeat:

1. Adding to the Word of God—asking for another's help when God does not require it (1:3);
2. Making commitments to others not authorized by the Word, e.g., "we will go with you" (1:3);
3. Taking from the Word—not fully carrying out divine orders as Saul did with Agag (1:4–7);
4. Depending more on human help than the Lord's help (1:17);
5. Settling with partial victory and tolerating the enemy (1:19);
6. Going into battle without an acknowledgment of God—prayerlessness (1:21).

On the other hand, to consider the positive side, we observe that the Lord's people are victorious when they act in faith. They do as follows:

1. Pray (1:1)
2. Obey (1:2)
3. Depend completely on the Lord (1:4)
4. Launch an offensive against the enemy (1:4, 8)
5. Continue their advances; they never stop short of victory (1:8, 9)
6. Accept the challenge (1:12–14)
7. Persevere until the victory is won

Regardless of the changing times, war or peace, God remains in absolute control of the nations. He acts compassionately, justly, and wisely. A careful study of action verbs proves this important point (e.g., 3:1, 7, 9, 10, 12, 15; 4:2, 9, 15, 23; 9:22, 57; 10:7; 13:1; 20:35). God is sovereign, Lord over all. He is in control of the nations. He will have the last word with them. He is the administrator of justice among His people and in the pagan world. He punishes the transgressors. Wars are an evidence of this. The basic cause of war is sin. He has mercy, however, on the repentant. He is a gracious, good God. This is learned from history. Learn your lessons.

Ruth: Trust Your Lord

R uth is the story of God's gracious, providential leading in the lives of His own people, some poor, some hurting, and some prosperous. This is whether they be a virtuous woman like Ruth, who comes to trust the God of Israel; a hurting wife and mother like Naomi, who knows something of deep sorrow; or an honorable man like Boaz, who is wealthy and trustworthy, deeply loving his Lord. Put this trusting combination together and watch what God produces: an ancestress in the lineage of our wonderful Lord.

The Book of Ruth vividly illustrates the truth of Romans 5:20: "But where sin increased, grace increased all the more." The setting for this historical narrative is the Book of Judges with its marching armies, its religious apostasy, and its self-centeredness. "Everyone did as he saw fit" (Judg. 21:25 NIV). In these turbulent times, the just and compassionate God freely gives His grace—the evidence being the Book of Ruth. Therefore this sacred record is like a breath of fresh air for people living in the smog of uncertainty and gloom.

Informational Material

Someone has observed that

> Judges and Samuel abound in scenes of lawlessness and strife. Armies march and countermarch. . . . There are scenes of savagery and lust. . . . In the Book of Ruth, however, the clash of arms and the tumult of men are strangely stilled. Here, one feels, is the life the people really lived.[15]

Behind the scenes there are traditional customs, courtship, marriage, and family.

This book is written sometime after the events occur, probably during the life of King David. It is read during the Feast of Weeks. The author is not named. Some suggest it may have been Samuel. The book is also referred to as an appendix or a supplement to Judges and an introduction to Samuel. This makes it an important book, for it confirms its historicity.

The purpose of the book is to trace the ancestry of David to Ruth the Moabitess. This introduces non-Israelite blood into the family line. The New Testament writer Matthew gives an account of the genealogy of Christ from Perez to David as stated in Ruth (Matt. 1:3–6; Ruth 4:18–22).

The book is accurate and true to facts as the author describes the customs of the people.

> It purports to be the account of something that actually happened. . . . The book also serves to show that the true religion is supranational and not confined to the bounds of any one people."[16] Archer concurs by saying, "It also teaches the far-reaching scope of the grace of

God, Who is ready to welcome even Gentile converts to the fellowship of His redeemed people.[17]

Ruth is a source of encouragement to trust God and to live for Him. Erdman says that this "charming romance . . . indicates the possibility of living in love and purity and peace even when surrounded by moral corruption and godlessness."[18]

Josephus, the Jewish historian, explains,

I was, therefore, obligated to relate this history of Ruth, because I had a mind to demonstrate the power of God, who without difficulty, can raise those that are of ordinary parentage to dignity and splendor, to which he advanced David, though he were born of such mean [average] parents."[19]

Brentius observes:

"With what wonderful compassion [does God raise] up the lowly and despised to the greatest glory and majesty."[20]

ANALYTICAL OVERVIEW

I. Introduction (1:1–5)
   A. Scene of action (1:1)
   B. Individuals involved (1:2)
   C. Sorrows experienced (1:3–5)
II. The return to Bethlehem (1:6–22)
   A. Incentive for returning (1:6)
   B. The sad farewell (1:7–14)
   C. Ruth's decision (1:15–18)
   D. Destination reached (1:19–22)

III. Ruth in the barley field (2:1–23)
 A. Desires to glean and find favor (2:1–3)
 B. Attracts the attention of Boaz (2:4–18)
 C. Reports to Naomi (2:19–23)
IV. The conversation at the threshing floor (3:1–18)
 A. Instruction from Naomi (3:1–5)
 B. Response of Boaz (3:6–15)
 C. Interaction with Naomi (3:16–18)
V. The marriage of Boaz and Ruth (4:1–22)
 A. Purchase of the land (4:1–8)
 B. Announcement made (4:9–12)
 C. Marriage consummated (4:13–22)

Practical Aspects

God has always had a people devoted to Him in life's darkest hours, and He always will. In times like those mentioned in the Book of Judges (Ruth 1:1), we might well ask the question: Where are the people of God in these dreadful days? The answer is simply: they are there, sparkling, shining, singing saints in a drab, defeated, and decaying society. Naomi, Ruth, and Boaz are individuals of quality character. In that generation they are the "light of the world" (Matt. 5:14).

Life has its sudden interruptions. Naomi does not expect her husband and two sons to die in Moab. Life never runs on an even keel. Often it is difficult to cope with—with its conflicts and complexities. Famine in Bethlehem takes Naomi to Moab, and while there, death of loved ones brings her sorrow. At long last she hears some good news that "the Lord had come to the aid of his people by providing food for them" (1:6 NIV). She sets out to return home.

In a corrupt society we would not expect to find deeds of kindness and words of spiritual significance. How refreshing to hear the vocabulary of the three principal characters and others. Listen to it: "May the Lord deal kindly with you" (1:8); "May the Lord grant that you may find rest" (1:9); "The hand of the Lord" (1:13); "The Almighty . . . the Lord . . . the Lord . . . the Almighty has afflicted me" (1:20–21); "May the Lord be with you" (2:4); "May the Lord bless you" (2:4); "May the Lord reward your work" (2:12); "May he who took notice of you be blessed" (2:19); "The Lord bless him" (2:20 NIV); "May you be blessed of the Lord" (3:10); "As the Lord lives" (3:13); "May the Lord make the woman . . ." (4:11); "Blessed is the Lord" (4:14). (The verses are from NASB.)

Ruth, a Moabitess with sterling and unblemished character, is now a worshiper of the God of Israel. Her faith is evident: "Your people will be my people, and your God, my God" (1:16). She is a woman of strong determination (1:18). I am impressed with her poise, polish, and politeness (2:7). She possesses humility and respect for others (2:10). She is known for her excellent reputation (3:12). She is not bored with life but is industrious and ambitious (2:2, 17, 18, 23). She is a loving daughter-in-law (4:15). This is the woman chosen of the Lord to be an ancestress of Jesus Christ, one saved out of heathen darkness to reflect His glory.

Finally, in looking at the example of Naomi, we see some timeless principles on how to handle hurts:

1. Make right decisions. Go to the place that is the will of God for your life (1:6)
2. Face up to reality—the reality of dead loved ones and of the needs of daughters-in-law (1:8–14)
3. Be gracious and submissive not bitter (1:9)

4. Focus on the welfare of others (1:8–14)
5. Don't be afraid to cry. Don't hold it in (1:9, 14)
6. Acknowledge your deep need in a confession (1:20-21)
7. Encourage others (2:1–7)
8. Recognize God's providential workings (2:20)
9. Trust your Lord

Looking to Jesus, accepting the reality of sorrow and suffering, and helping others goes a long way in handling your hurts.

1 Samuel: Cherish Your Calling

The Books of Samuel reveal the background of an administrative change of leadership in Israel's government. Heretofore, Moses, Joshua, and then the judges are the heads of the nation. Now Israel desires a king of its own.

This historical account of Samuel is important to the people of God because it tells why and how the nation moves from a theocracy (a government under God by immediate divine guidance) to a monarchy (undivided rule or absolute sovereignty by a single person). Thus—in addition to the Israelites—Samuel, Saul, and David play a prominent role in this story.

INFORMATIONAL MATERIAL

The Hebrew Bible regards these two volumes as one book; the same is true of 1 and 2 Kings. The Septuagint translation divides the book into two parts, calling them "The First and Second Books of the Kingdom."

The human authors are Samuel and perhaps several others. According to 1 Chronicles 29:29, these books are a compilation of several writers: Samuel, Nathan, and Gad. Samuel could not have written the entire book because it tells of his death (25:1). "The fact that the books were named for Samuel indicates the high honor in which he was held."[21]

Samuel means "name of God" or "a godly name." Samuel himself is a praying judge with a prophetic gift (7:15). He is the last of the judges (Acts 13:20; 3:24). Therefore, in a sense, he is the bridge between the judges and the prophets because he is both judge and prophet.

Some think of him as a priest (2:18). His father is from the tribe of Ephraim (1:1) not Levi. His early life, spent in the house of the Lord in Shiloh, gives him a priestly perspective. Later he becomes judge. Living in Ramah, he embarks on a circuit from Bethel to Gilgal to Mizpah, judging Israel in all those places (7:16 NIV).

In a time setting, Samuel is three hundred years from Moses. Some have suggested that the events mentioned in 1 Samuel cover a period of about one hundred years (c. 1050 to 950 B.C.).

ANALYTICAL OVERVIEW

I. The life and ministry of Samuel (1:1–7:17)
    A. Born of a praying mother (1:1–2:10)
    B. Ministers in the temple (2:11–36)
    C. Hears God speak (3:1–21)
    D. Lives in turbulent times (4:1–7:1)
    E. Judges Israel many years (7:2–17)
II. The selection and rejection of Saul (8:1–15:35)
    A. Israel requests a king (8:1–22)
    B. Samuel anoints Saul (9:1–11:15)
    C. Samuel's farewell message (12:1–25)
    D. Saul's impatience and failure (13:1–23)
    E. Israel's victories (14:1–52)

F. Saul's disobedience and rejection (15:1–35)
III. The selection and preservation of David (16:1–31:13)
    A. Anointed by Samuel (16:1–23)
    B. Overcomes Goliath (17:1–58)
    C. Object of Saul's hostility (18:1–20:42)
    D. Wanders in many places (21:1–30:31)
    E. Saul's final battle and death (31:1–13)

PRACTICAL ASPECTS

This book tells us that God answers prayer. He answers prayer for Hannah and gives her Samuel (1:12–17, 25–28); for Samuel and grants victory over the Philistines (7:9; cf. 8:6–7; 12:18, 23); for David and gives him guidance (23:1–4, 10–12; 30:8).

The Lord preserves His own. The child Samuel lives in a religious environment of abominable and sordid hypocrisy: The priests are disobedient in the matter of presenting offerings to God; they are guilty of gross immorality (2:22); they are disobedient to their father, Eli, the priest (2:25). God keeps Samuel; "the boy grew up in the presence of the Lord" (2:21).

What do we do when we are confronted by a critical situation and we feel pressure? Do we hide? Run away? Do something rash or stupid? Become fearful? (13:6–10) Saul becomes fearful, pushes the panic button, becomes unglued, and acts out of fear rather than on the Word of God.

One should not act out of fear in a crisis; act on the Word of God. Wait on the Lord and be patient. "They shall not be ashamed who wait for me" (Isa. 49:23 KJV). On the other hand, we can launch out in faith. Jonathan did (14:6–15). In so doing, God puts the enemy on the run.

Cherish your calling. Have a high regard for what God asks you to do. First Samuel shows us the strengths and weaknesses of men. In times of turbulence, God seeks to mold a man for His work. He takes a dedicated boy, Samuel, and makes him a judge and prophet. He takes a shepherd boy, David, and makes him a king.

This is what God can do. Let Him work through you.

2 Samuel: Discharge Your Duties

Second Samuel continues the historical narrative of 1 Samuel in presenting a record of events occurring in David's life before and after his ascendancy to the throne. It is a revelation of God's providential and disciplinary workings in the king's life and of the king carrying out his duties under God.

> The first book of Samuel closes with the introduction of David. We saw him in preparation for his life work: in the fields as a shepherd; in the palace as musician and courtier; in the wilderness as outlaw. He was fitted for the position to which he was appointed and for which he had been anointed. In the second book, we have the history of his specific work to the purpose of God.[22]

Keep in mind that the Hebrew Bible regards these two books, 1 and 2 Samuel, as one single book.

INFORMATIONAL MATERIAL

Young states that:

> these chapters are specimens of noble Hebrew prose, and from the literary standpoint alone may be regarded as incomparable masterpieces. . . . The trustworthiness and historical character of the books of Samuel is seen from the fact that they are alluded to in other portions of the sacred Scriptures (e.g., 1 Kings 2:27, 1 Chron. 23, Jer., and Psalm 17).[23]

Jesus Himself refers to David who eats the consecrated showbread (Matt. 12:3–4). Paul refers to Samuel when he preaches in the synagogue in Antioch (Acts 13:20–22).

Although the emphasis of 2 Samuel is on historical events, it is important to note that such information gives insight into the character of David the king. What David says or does in these various situations indicates the kind of person he really is. Many of the events recorded are indeed sad or exhilarating, tragic or even gruesome, and are not really understood by Christians walking in New Testament light. Nevertheless, as we go beneath the surface, we discover that David is certainly a man after God's own heart, who longs to do God's will (Acts 13:22). For example:

1. He is a man of tenderness, tears, and compassion. He weeps over his enemies (1:17) and shows kindness to them (2:6). He weeps over his rebellious son who has broken his heart (18:5, 33).
2. With God in his thoughts, David is a man of faith, for he waits on Him with sincere prayer (5:19; 7:18).

3. He is a man of generosity, big-hearted, and blesses his people not only with words but also with gifts (6:18–19).
4. He is a man with brokenness of spirit. After having sinned against God, confessing his sin (12:13), fasting and praying (12:16–17), he accepts God's righteous discipline without bitterness and with transparent humility.
5. David possesses strong emotions as he worships the Lord with all his heart, celebrating, singing, leaping, and dancing before Him (6:5,14–15).

Rightly does Morgan say of him:

There were times when faith faltered, and he did foolish things, when his passion mastered him, when he fell into fearful sin; but underneath the faltering faith, I find a faith that never faltered; deeper than the passion was the passionate desire for holiness; profounder than any sin, however heinous, was the attitude of soul which could say, 'My soul followeth hard after God.'[24]

God gave us these books to serve as a warning, instruction, and encouragement (Rom. 15:4; 1 Cor. 10:11).

ANALYTICAL OVERVIEW

I. Events before David's kingship (1:1–5:5)
    A. The death of Saul (1:1–27)
    B. Men of Judah anoint David (2:1–7)
    C. Conflict between houses of David and Saul (2:8–4:12)
    D. Men of Israel anoint David (5:1–5)
II. Events during David's kingship (5:6–22:51)
    A. David's success (5:6–10:19)
    B. David's fall and restoration (11:1–12:31)

    C. David's suffering (13:1–21:22)
    D. David's song (22:1–51)
  III. Events at the close of David's kingship (23:1–24:25)
    A. The recording of his last words (23:1–7)
    B. The listing of mighty men (23:8–39)
    C. The taking of a census (24:1–25)

PRACTICAL ASPECTS

The Lord does not give the throne to David immediately after he wins a major military victory over Goliath and the Philistines. Instant fulfillment of a promise involving heavy responsibilities is nowhere taught in the Scriptures. We do not rise to spiritual stardom after we consecrate our lives to Christ and are filled with His Spirit. We may be on our way, but we still have not arrived.

It neither happens to David, nor to Moses, nor to Paul. Paul lives in years of obscurity in Tarsus, his hometown, long before the Spirit of God launches him out in missionary journeys. This is preceded by three years in the desert. The Holy Spirit always prepares His man for years before He permits him to carry a leader's load.

It takes time to build a firm foundation of spiritual quality in our lives. There is no instant maturity. Acting in TV shows, playing as a star on a pro football team, or participating in the political arena does not qualify us. God is not in a hurry to use our lives.

The authentic servant of the Lord is put through many tests, often over a long period of time. Do not be impatient. If God does not fulfill His promise overnight, do not collapse or worry. He will fulfill it in His time. Wait on Him.

Saul's impatience and disobedience cost him the throne. David's patience and obedience carry him to the throne. David does not seek it. The tribes of Israel and Judah come to put him there. God is not looking for ability but availability.

The Lord increases our strength "little by little." David becomes "more and more powerful" (5:10 NIV). "David grew stronger and stronger while the house of Saul grew weaker and weaker" (3:1 NIV). The Holy Spirit continuously fills the believer (Eph. 5:18).

Peter is filled with the Holy Spirit on the day of Pentecost (Acts 2), but we read of him again being filled with the Holy Spirit as he faces a new crisis: "Peter, filled with the Holy Spirit" (Acts 4:8). John the Baptizer preaches, "He [God] gives the Spirit without measure" (John 3:34). There is no end nor limit to how much we may receive from the Holy Spirit.

1 Kings: Know Your History

History is a graphic picture of the past. This is what life looks like in that segment of time of 120 to 125 years, from King Solomon to King Ahaziah. While observing key players and significant events in this historical narrative, we are deeply moved. We see the golden age of Solomon and the black smudge in the reign of Ahaz. These pictures have realities of both beauty and tragedy.

First Kings is a part of the historical records preserved for the people of Israel and for us. In it, we note royalty and the commoner, peace and war, faith and unbelief, the true and the false prophet, blessing and judgment, that which is right and that which is wrong in God's sight.

Additionally, knowing history, whether it be sacred or secular, helps us understand where we are today as a people and a nation under God. We need the past to interpret the present and to have insight into the future. First Kings assists us in avoiding what is wrong and in clinging to what is right.

INFORMATIONAL MATERIAL

Originally 1 and 2 Kings comprised one volume. Later the volume was divided into two books, largely for convenience, and without any change or loss of content. No one knows who wrote Kings. Some think, without evidence, that Jeremiah is the author.

Jesus and New Testament writers are acquainted with Kings. For example, Jesus Himself speaks of Solomon several times. In the Sermon on the Mount, Jesus recognizes "Solomon in all his glory" (Matt. 6:29). While speaking to scribes and Pharisees, Jesus declares, "One greater than Solomon is here" (Matt. 12:42). Luke writes of the widows in the days of Elijah (Luke 4:25–26). Paul calls attention to the "seven thousand who have not bowed the knee to Baal" (Rom. 11:2–5). James uses Elijah as a model "pray-er" (James 5:17–18).

The many prophets so prominently mentioned throughout the book are a visible evidence of God's presence among His people. He does not abandon them in the dark days of abounding sin. He continually speaks to them through the prophets, proving that God is the Lord of love, grace, mercy, goodness, and justice, as well as the One of judgment in the administration of His government among the sons of men.

First Kings is an eloquent testimony to the faithfulness of God. He is true to His Word. What He says, He does without fail. He can be trusted.

ANALYTICAL OVERVIEW

I. The kingdom united (1:1–11:43)
   A. Solomon selected as king (1:1–2:46)
   B. The Lord's first revelation to Solomon (3:1–28)
   C. The kingdom established (4:1–34)
   D. The building of the temple (5:1–7:51)
   E. The temple dedicated (8:1–66)
   F. The Lord's second revelation to Solomon (9:1–9)

Practical Aspects

Have you ever been discouraged? Someone has rightly said, "No one is immune to the problem of discouragement, . . . not even those who are spiritually mature and considered successful." Elijah is an excellent example of this truth, and like him, we get discouraged because we see only the dark side.

But there is a bright side. God is gracious in His dealings with the discouraged, being compassionate, patient, and strong. He allows Elijah to come to the end of himself, to wind down and fall asleep. When we come to this point, the Lord begins to do something for us. Elijah is ready to receive. He has exhausted his resources.

Like Elijah, every discouraged person needs a physical touch. God knows this. Sometimes discouragement may be the result of a weakened physical condition. Elijah is tired and fearful; therefore, God lets him sleep. Sleep is good therapy. It is refreshing, renewing, and strengthening. We know how good we feel after a night of rest.

Not only does an exhausted, discouraged person need rest and sleep, but also he needs food. How considerate God is to dispatch an angel to give Elijah bread baked over hot coals and a jar of water. This is repeated a second time. He is strengthened physically. God does not forsake him when he is depressed.

Like Elijah, every discouraged person on the way to wholeness and hope needs not only a physical touch but also spiritual renewal. The Lord follows Elijah to a cave—his refuge, his place of safety—and speaks to him. How wonderful to hear from heaven. When God speaks, He does not lecture nor chastise him. He asks Elijah a question, without condemning or making him feel guilty.

It is therapeutic to ventilate our feelings. This acts as a catharsis for our souls. We need to express ourselves. When Elijah speaks, he magnifies his problems. This is characteristic of those who are depressed. Things are not as bad as we think they are.

After allowing His prophet to ventilate, the Lord says to Elijah, "Go forth and stand on the mountain before the Lord." It is as if He is saying, "Get out of the cave, Elijah. I did not make you for the cave. The cave is too confining. It is dark and gloomy. I want you to climb the mountain, exert yourself, take a breath of fresh air. Get a vision of My majesty and magnificence."

God does not make us for the cave—that room of gloom, doom, and self-pity—and to live in isolation. We are to climb the mountain and hear Him. There is a time to eat and sleep and a time to get out of our cozy cave.

On the mountain God sent a dazzling display of His power—wind, earthquake, and fire—but these do not speak to Elijah. Afterward comes "a sound of gentle blowing"

(NASB), "a still small voice" (KJV), "a gentle whisper" (NIV). It is that deep inner consciousness of sweet assurance: God is.

Elijah is humbled. The power of discouragement is broken. Little by little he is being healed. God strengthens him physically and spiritually. Now he is able to continue in service for his Lord. Discouragement is conquered.

2 Kings: Give Your Witness

To some history is indeed a significant subject to study; to others, boring. Some appreciate it; others ignore or despise it. Whatever your attitude, I suggest you take time to read Kings. It could change your thinking as it portrays real life, sometimes beautiful and sometimes ugly. It is a fast-moving account, covering a period of approximately four hundred years from Solomon to the fall of Jerusalem.

You will be amazed as you read of Elijah being carried to heaven in a chariot of fire or the miracle of the floating ax head as the power of God works through the prophet Elisha. You will also become aware of the depravity of sinful mankind without God, given over to intense hatred and violence. You will concur with Jeremiah who said, "The heart is deceitful above all things, and desperately wicked; who can know it?" (Jer. 17:9 NKJV).

Finally, you cannot fail to notice the goodness of God again and again as He seeks to hold together a nation in rebellion against Him. After hundreds of years of mercies extended, He finally gives them over to their captors. This is 2 Kings.

Informational Material

First and Second Kings yield important background facts for several Old Testament books. Isaiah and Micah prophesy during the reign of Uzziah, Jotham, Ahaz, and Hezekiah. These are the prophets sent to Judah, the southern kingdom. Isaiah is mentioned by name in 2 Kings 19:2.

In the northern kingdom, Israel—sometimes referred to as Samaria or Ephraim—Elijah and Elisha are the spokesmen for God for many years. Second Kings makes mention of Jonah, who wrote the book bearing his name (14:25). Amos and Hosea prophesy during the reign of Jereboam II (Amos 1:1; Hos. 1:1). Spiritual enlightenment comes to the kingdoms, both to the southern and the northern, through these men of God.

The witness of the mighty miracles and words of Elijah and Elisha, followed by the five contemporary prophets—Isaiah, Micah, Jonah, Amos, and Hosea—gives proof that the Lord deeply desires to fulfill His promise both to David (1 Kings 2:2–4) and to his son Solomon (1 Kings 9:2–9). For centuries, everything possible is done to influence the kings to obey the word of the Lord. They refuse to listen; consequently, the kingdoms are destroyed. Sin does its deadly work and takes its toll.

In order to complete the picture of life during the reigns of the kings, read the writings of the above mentioned contemporary prophets. Kings provides an overview of the political life of the times, whereas the prophecies reveal spiritual conditions in the kingdom.

ANALYTICAL OVERVIEW

I. The kingdom of Israel (1:1–17:41)
    A. The activity and departure of Elijah (1:1–2:11)
    B. The impact of Elisha's ministry (2:12–9:10)
    C. The work of judgment through Jehu (9:11–10:36)
    D. The reign of kings of Israel and Judah synchronized (11:1–16:20)
    E. The fall of Israel (17:1–41)
II. The kingdom of Judah (18:1–25:30)
    A. The reign of Hezekiah (18:1–20:21)
    B. The reign of Manasseh (21:1–18)
    C. The reign of Amon (21:19–26)
    D. The reign of Josiah (22:1–23:30)
    E. The reign of Judah's last kings (23:31–25:7)
    F. The fall of Judah (25:8–30)

PRACTICAL ASPECTS

The principles of divine justice found in Kings enable us to trace the rise and fall of a nation. There are specific reasons why this takes place. When the Lord is acknowledged and served, the nation is on the rise. When He is forsaken, and leaders and people serve other gods, they are destined for a fall. It is just that simple. Kings gives evidence of this unchanging truth. Look at America in this light.

It has been said that "the mills of God grind slow, but they grind exceedingly fine" and "God moves with a leaden foot, but strikes with an iron hand." These expressions indicate that Almighty God does not carry out His work of judgment immediately. He allots a grace period during which time He speaks in love and with patience. How long this lasts is known only to Him. Therefore, it is important for the transgressors to respond to His call lest they become objects of His righteous judgments.

When the days of grace come to an end and a decision is made, God steps in and does the work He is so reluctant to do—judge with finality. He cannot do otherwise for He is just and holy. This is the unchanging God of the Old and New Testaments.

Departure from God creates an environment of sin. This is the work of a depraved and rebellious mankind. God deals with it by raising up prophets and various people to live in these appalling conditions and to witness for Him. Their impressive testimonies to society declare forthrightly: God is! This is why the Lord saved you and me and continues to keep us here in this sinful world that we might be His mouthpiece to lead straying souls to Him. This is grace, God's marvelous grace revealed in His witnesses.

Be His witness. He will not only use your personal testimony while you are living, but after you die it will continue speaking (Heb. 11:4). For your encouragement, consider the nameless young girl's sincere witness given to her mistress (2 Kings 5:3). It sets off a chain of events from her to Naaman, commander of the Syrian Army, to the king of Syria, to the king of Israel, to Elisha the prophet, resulting in a miracle of healing. Who knows how far-reaching your witness for Jesus Christ will go?

1 Chronicles: Win Your Battle

For a fast-moving, pacesetting, space-age generation, genealogy is usually not one's cup of tea. To such, it is meaningless. On the other hand there are those who revel in such a study. What may be drab and dull for one is bright and stimulating for another.

First Chronicles contains much genealogical material. Many books of the Bible include some of the same: Genesis, Exodus, Numbers, Ruth, 2 Samuel, 2 Kings, Ezra, Nehemiah, Matthew, and Luke. Therefore genealogy is important.

Reading 1 Chronicles may not be interesting at first glance, but upon careful study, significant gems of truth appear, many of which we are not aware. This book begins with Adam and closes with the death of David. It spans the centuries with genealogy and centers on the reign of King David, who seeks to lead his people toward God with praise and joy.

INFORMATIONAL MATERIAL

Chronicles, much like Kings, is originally one manuscript in the Jewish canon. Upon being translated into the

Greek, it is divided into two volumes. Our English version follows the same form. Chronicles means "the words of the day." It is a historical record.

The authorship of Chronicles is uncertain. Some think, with good reason, that Ezra the scribe is the author. This much is true: The closing sentences of 2 Chronicles are the first sentences of Ezra (2 Chron. 36:22–23; Ezra 1:1–3).

Genealogical lists are not only given in the first nine chapters of Chronicles, but they are also found throughout the book: chapters 11, 12, 14, 15, 23, 24, 25, 26, 27. This emphasis on genealogy, I personally believe, reveals God's love and concern for the individual and the family. They are identifiable persons with names, privileges, and responsibilities for a purpose in the plan of God. Genealogy connects the generations, the present with the past.

The second main division of Chronicles deals with the reign of King David, who is "a man after God's own heart." David is a spiritually sensitive man. His concerns are for God, the ark, and the temple, and for the people in his kingdom, that they might be rightly related to Him in faith and obedience.

Moreover, David is courageous, zealous, prayerful. It is true: he fails God by sinning, but in repenting and receiving forgiveness, he learns his lessons. Henceforth, he does not continue to practice what he knows is not right. He is obedient to God at all costs.

As a man of praise, David makes good use of music in worship, which is an expression of joy in the Lord. Singers and musicians are selected by him "for the service of the house of God" (1 Chron. 25:6–8). Authentic worship is a reverential and joyful experience.

ANALYTICAL OVERVIEW

I. The records of genealogy (1:1–9:44)
   A. Descendants of Adam (1:1–26)
   B. Descendants of Abraham (1:27–2:2)
   C. Descendants of Judah (2:3–55)
   D. Descendants of David (3:1–24)
   E. Descendants of Judah, Simeon, Reuben, Gad, Manasseh (4:1–5:26)
   F. Descendants of Levi (6:1–81)
   G. Descendants of Issachar, Benjamin, Naphtali, Manasseh, Ephraim, Asher (7:1–8:40)
   H. Inhabitants of Jerusalem (9:1–44)
II. The reign of David (10:1–29:30)
   A. Begins after Saul's death (10:1–14)
   B. Anointed king over Israel (11:1–12:40)
   C. Brings the ark to Jerusalem (13:1–16:43)
   D. Desires to build the temple (17:1–27)
   E. Wins military victories (18:1–20:8)
   F. Transgresses the law (21:1–30)
   G. Prepares for building the temple (22:1–19)
   H. Organizes the kingdom (23:1–27:34)
   I. Addresses the final assembly (28:1–29:30)

PRACTICAL ASPECTS

Life in the twentieth century is strikingly similar to what it was in the days of Saul and David. The contrast between these two men is reflected in every generation of society, including ours. Saul is a man of the flesh—one who lives without a sensitiveness toward God—impulsive, jealous, hateful, disobedient, and totally dependent on self. David, a man of the Spirit, seeks to walk with God, being submissive to His will. Through life's experiences a spiritual maturity is developed in him. Check yourself. Are you a man or woman of the flesh or of the Spirit? This is the difference between life and death, victory and defeat.

Our Lord uses various processes to accomplish His purposes in us, with us, and for us. He does not reveal in advance the ingredients for making up that process. It is not to be discovered through a secret formula. Actually, it is a series of divine workings, often unknown to us, with a divine objective in mind. Patiently, silently, providentially, personally, and perfectly the Lord brings us to the place where He wants us to be. This is not done overnight.

Our part in the process is to be submissive and sensitive to Him. We are to trust and obey. God has a plan in mind for David. He is to be king over Israel. He is destined for the throne. In His time, through His process, the Lord gets him there, taking him from the pasture to the palace. Little by little, this is accomplished.

Keep in mind that during the process we may experience a heartbreaking defeat or an unexpected loss. David did, and so may we if we fail to act on the Word of God. In bringing the ark to Jerusalem, he did not follow divine instructions; consequently, he is deeply hurt. Through his pain, there comes a change of heart. Now he seeks God first. He learns that in carrying out God's will, he is to do it His way. For God's work done in God's way will always have God's approval. Are you putting the Lord first?

Yes, all of us have our battles and our blessings. First Chronicles gives us a number of principles that will help us to win over our struggles: (1) live with an awareness of God; (2) cultivate a praiseful spirit; (3) settle for nothing less than God's best—His will; (4) cooperate with others since teamwork is essential to triumph; (5) always remember that success never comes easily; (6) after the victory, keep up your guard; and (7) envision the future and prepare for it.

2 Chronicles: Understand Your Times

Biblical history teems with excitement. It deals with the unpredictable human personality factor. It tells of critical and crucial situations, matters of life and death. It traces the movements of divine sovereignty that cannot be detected with the human eye nor recorded on its pages. History has mystery as well as exposure. Becoming a student of it will make one wiser.

In 2 Chronicles, we see the rise and fall of a kingdom, the good and bad of a reigning king, the joys of a right relationship with God, and the sorrows and sufferings of turning away from Him. This historical record helps us to understand our present times, and it is beneficial in planning for the future.

Second Chronicles continues the narrative of 1 Chronicles, beginning with the reign of Solomon and closing with the proclamation of Cyrus. It covers over four hundred years.

INFORMATIONAL MATERIAL

The emphasis of 2 Chronicles is on the Davidic line of kings. The impact of David's life is felt throughout the book, especially in the life of his son Solomon. David's name is mentioned seventy-three times with reference to his person, his words, his work, and his city, Jerusalem.

The Lord promises David the continuation of his throne through Solomon and his posterity (2 Sam. 7:12–16). It is made clear to both David and Solomon that obedience to the Word of God and loyalty to Him are of prime importance—a must. Should the Lord be forsaken, He will uproot the kingdom and remove the people from the land (2 Chron. 7:19–22).

Tragically, this comes to pass; but not before the Lord shows great mercy, patience, compassion, and restraint over many years of rebellion and abominable practices of both kings and people. Throughout this entire period, He is never without many witnesses. His Spirit-inspired prophets and godly priests live among the people. Moreover, they have "the book of the law of the Lord" (2 Chron. 34:14–21).

A fuller picture of this period of history may be gained by reading the Books of Jeremiah and Zephaniah. The prophet Jeremiah is with the nation until the very end. Yet God gives him a vision beyond the end. He sees the restoration of the people to their land after seventy years of captivity. How gracious and good God is.

ANALYTICAL OVERVIEW

I. The reign of Solomon (1:1–9:31)
    A. The building of the temple (1:1–4:22)

PRACTICAL ASPECTS

The expression, "but a prophet of the Lord was there," has at times burned like fire in my soul (28:9 NASB). It tells me that in turbulent times God has His man in the middle of them. Such a man, sent from Him, is always in the right place at the right time. In the sovereignty of God, time, place, and persons all blend together for the purpose of advancing His cause and kingdom. I want to be His man—wherever He puts me.

After reading Chronicles, ask yourself this question: What makes a nation great? Is it her military might, her intellectual capabilities, her Olympic champions, her commerce and industry? I think not. A nation is great when God is close to it, acknowledged, worshiped, and obeyed. Certainly, Solomon discovers this to be true, which is in keeping with the word of Moses: "For what nation is there so great, who hath *God so nigh unto them* as the Lord our God is in all things that we call upon Him for?" (Deut. 4:7 KJV, italics added).

A nation loses its greatness when it turns away from the Lord and His Word. It may become unfaithful in its prosperity and coast on the momentum of the past, taking too much for granted. Continuing in the slide away from God, the nation becomes careless and indifferent and looks in another direction to a false god. Little by little, moral and spiritual erosion sets in and greatness dies within the nation.

To counteract the downward spiral of the nation, the Spirit of the Lord continues His dynamic working, coming on Azariah (15:1). This is proof of His powerful ministry in Old Testament times. How encouraging! The Holy Spirit has full knowledge of what is happening, where and why it takes place, and who is involved. He knows everything there is to know in advance of every happening. He is always up to date in His workings. He is never to be outdone, outmatched, outmaneuvered, or outthought. He is aggressive but not brash; always tactful. He is never at a loss as to what to do. The Holy Spirit is in today's world. Depend on Him.

This is the Christian's joy—to have God's presence with us. During the days of John Wesley, the Methodists often used the expression, "The best of all is that God is with us." Amen!

Ezra: Pack Your Bags

There comes a special moment in the life of a Christian when God says, "It is time to move. Pack your bags and get going." This is what is happening in the historical account of Ezra as he writes of the return of the exiles to Jerusalem. The proclamation of Cyrus is heard throughout Persia where the news of freedom is received gratefully by those who have longed for their homeland over the many years.

The day to return arrives. There are 42,360 packing up and ready to go. With mingled feelings, they set out on their journey and reach their destination after months of travel over dusty roads. They are home at last.

This does not "just happen." God plans for the return of the exiles years before. His sovereignty and faithfulness now make this a reality. The Book of Ezra gives us a glimpse of His gracious workings.

INFORMATIONAL MATERIAL

Ezra, the author of this book, is the principal personality. Having written the history of the first return of the exiles, he then tells of his own personal involvement in the second return to Jerusalem. As a priest and scribe, he writes with clarity and honesty, giving a few details of significant actions. He carries out his various responsibilities in keeping with the law of the Lord. His account begins where 2 Chronicles ends—the decree of Cyrus.

Like Luke, the Gospel writer, Ezra also uses a number of sources of information for his book: the proclamations of kings, tables of genealogy, letters of correspondence, reports, and decrees. This is evidence that both writers are exacting investigators of historical facts (cf. Luke 1:1–4). Nothing is written by them that is not true.

In gaining an understanding of Ezra, it is necessary to keep in mind chronology. The book opens with the proclamation of Cyrus given in 538 B.C. After twenty-three years, the rebuilt temple is finished in 515 B.C. This is followed by a time gap of fifty-seven years. A second return under Ezra begins in 458 B.C.; therefore, the book covers approximately eighty years.[25]

Ezra, a deeply spiritual man whose ancestry goes back to Aaron, is one upon whom God's hand rests. "He set his heart to study the law of the Lord, and to practice it, and to teach His statutes and ordinances in Israel" (7:10 NASB). His priestly office and scribal ability qualify him for spiritual leadership to the exiles in their return to Jerusalem.

Ezra catches the eye of King Artaxerxes, who places upon him the responsibility of stewardship of resources for temple use. In addition to the qualities of integrity and dependability, Ezra possesses a heart of humility and compassion as he prays with a sense of unworthiness for the residents of the land who have grieved God by pagan intermarriages. He institutes reforms to correct the wrongs.

The Book of Ezra is an important link in the chain of Jewish history.

ANALYTICAL OVERVIEW

I. The first return to Jerusalem under Zerubbabel (1:1–6:22)
   A. The proclamation of Cyrus (1:1–4)
   B. The response of those in exile (1:5–2:70)
   C. The assembly in Jerusalem (3:1–6)
   D. The work of the temple begun (3:7–13)
   E. The hindrances of the adversaries (4:1–24)
   F. The work on the temple resumed and finished (5:1–6:22)
II. The second return to Jerusalem under Ezra (7:1–10:44)
   A. The leadership of Ezra (7:1–10)
   B. The decree of Artaxerxes (7:11–28)
   C. The journey to Jerusalem (8:1–36)
   D. The prayer and reforms of Ezra (9:1–10:44)

PRACTICAL ASPECTS

Throughout the latter part of the book, Ezra uses a very significant expression a number of times: "the hand of God," indicating that God is at work in him, in others, and in all that is happening. The Sovereign Lord makes possible the return to Jerusalem, working through pagan kings and His own people.

Well did Morgan put it:

The principle revealed is that God presses into His service men who do not know Him, and who are unconscious that they are carrying out His will; and inspires men who do know Him, and compels them to constructive activity.[26]

The return of the exiles is not something taking place by chance but by the divine decree. God plans and determines it. He does all things well because He knows what to do, how to do it, and when it is to be done. God's hand upon us results in blessing, direction, and assurance.

Before and after God does great things for us, we have the responsibility of being faithful and true to Him. One of the dark scenes in this bright picture is that some of those who return to their homeland allow the culture of surrounding nations to divert them from the ways of the Lord. Becoming unfaithful, they enter into unlawful marriage relationships. The pressures of the times are too great for them. Are they for you?

This is why it is so vitally important to daily live close to our Lord and to have His hand of blessing upon us, to strengthen us to go against the current of public opinion. Human nature is too weak to overcome worldly influences. We need divine life and daily grace, which are always available to us.

Nehemiah: Fulfill Your Responsibility

The Book of Nehemiah tells us a lot about people and how God works through them to accomplish His purposes. Nehemiah himself is one of those whom his Lord uses to carry out the monumental task of rebuilding the walls and gates of Jerusalem and to bring renewal and joy to the returned exiles in spiritual need.

His historical account begins on a distressing note as he hears the report from his brother, who tells him of conditions in the holy city. After a time of weeping, fasting, and praying, Nehemiah goes to the king and receives permission to go to Jerusalem. While there he mobilizes many to assist in the construction of the walls. Encountering severe opposition, he—with all the workers—persists in fulfilling his responsibilities, and the walls and gates are finished.

These activities are followed by a large assembly that is given to the reading of the law, the confession of sin, and an acknowledgment of God's greatness and goodness. After these things, a joyous dedication of the Jerusalem wall is held. The book closes with a series of reforms initiated by Nehemiah and a sentence prayer: "Remember me, O my God, for good" (13:31).

INFORMATIONAL MATERIAL

It is not specifically mentioned in Scripture where Nehemiah is born, but from facts of history and chronology, apparently he is a child of exiled parents living in Persia. How he comes to the place of prominence in King Artaxerxes' court is not known. His position as cupbearer indicates he is close to the king as one of his trusted servants; thus he is a person of integrity.

From his book, we discover that godliness characterizes his life. He prays day and night as he humbles himself before God, confessing his sins and those of his father's house (1:6). He prays when he is in serious conversation with the king (2:4b). Facing the opposition of the enemy, he prays (4:9; 6:14). In his daily tasks he acknowledges his Lord (5:19; 13:14, 22, 29). He lives as being in God's presence. This spiritual leader is the writer of this historical book.

A man of sterling character, Nehemiah is made governor in the land of Judah (5:14). His unselfishness is quite evident. He makes no demands on the people in their impoverished condition to supply his needs (5:17–18). In his leadership role, he labors alongside his workers untiringly, giving of himself (4:23). He believes God for victory in the struggle against the enemies (4:20).

Nehemiah goes to Jerusalem in 444 B.C., and, after a twelve year period, he returns to Persia. It is not known how much time he spends there. At a later date he goes back to Jerusalem (13:6–7).

One of the unusual features of the book is the mention of so many names. Does not this indicate that God is concerned about individuals? Not one escapes His all-seeing eye. Ezra, the priest and scribe, has a very important ministry during these times also.

ANALYTICAL OVERVIEW

I. The rebuilding of the wall and gates of Jerusalem (1:1–7:73)
    A. Concerns and prayer of Nehemiah (1:1–11)
    B. Arrival and observations of the city (2:1–20)
    C. Rebuilding begun (3:1–32)
    D. Opposition overcome (4:1–23)
    E. Internal problems solved (5:1–19)
    F. Enemies outsmarted (6:1–14)
    G. Work completed (6:15–7:3)
    H. Genealogical records found (7:4–73)
II. The renewal of the people (8:1–12:47)
    A. The reading of the law by Ezra (8:1–8)
    B. The joy of the people (8:9–18)
    C. The prayer offered (9:1–38)
    D. The agreement made (10:1–39)
    E. The list of people, priests, and Levites (11:1–12:26)
    F. The dedication of the wall (12:27–47)
III. The reforms of Nehemiah (13:1–31)
    A. Concerning Tobiah (13:1–9)
    B. Concerning the Levites (13:10–14)
    C. Concerning the Sabbath (13:15–22)
    D. Concerning unlawful marriages (13:23–31)

PRACTICAL ASPECTS

One's best days are those spent in a close relationship with the Lord. There is nothing higher, finer, or sweeter. This reminds me of the time when I asked a man who waited on me while making a purchase, "Did you say your prayers this morning?" He was taken aback by that question, but it opened the door to a conversation about Jesus Christ.

I discovered that at one time he was a professing Christian. As I reminded him of the blessedness of that life in Christ, his eyes filled with tears. He remembered those days when he was right with his Lord. They were his best.

I wish I could say that he came back to the Savior at that time, but I do not know what happened after I left the store. I was a stranger in that town.

The returned exiles also weep when they hear the Word of God being read by Ezra and explained to them in a great assembly in Jerusalem (8:1–9). They receive it and obey it; the result is "great rejoicing" (8:17). They learn by experience that the promise given to them is true: "The joy of the Lord is your strength" (8:10).

God speaks to us through His Word; therefore, read it daily with faith, and it will add to your joy. Years before, the prophet Jeremiah declared: "Thy words were found and I ate them, and Thy words became for me a joy and the delight of my heart" (Jer. 15:16).

The incomparable Word of the Lord does many wonderful things for us. It adds to our joys, enriches our relationship with Him, and strengthens us for His service.

Esther: Recall Your Rescue

This book is packed with excitement, the breathtaking issues of life and death, and the reality of bad news and good news. In times such as these, what should be done? The thrilling story of Queen Esther and Mordecai in a pagan empire offers us insights for taking proper actions in the hour of crisis.

The bad news for the Jewish exiles is that they are to be destroyed—both young and old, women and children—on a designated day. All they ever owned will be plundered by the murderers. Indeed, the outlook is gloomy.

But the good news is that there are two Jews who have the courage to confront the evil. Queen Esther is willing to lay her life on the line as she is given sound instructions by Mordecai. In the providence of God, both are used to turn the tables on wicked Haman and his plans, and the Jews' brush with death is over. They have a victory celebration.

The institution of the Feast of Purim still observed by Jews today, is the outcome of these unforgettable events of history. In this manner, they recall their rescue.

Informational Material

It is not known who wrote the Book of Esther. After reading it a number of times, I am wondering if Mordecai may have written it. This is only a supposition. He had the ability to write a decree for the kingdom of Persia, backed by the authority of the king (8:8). He was a gifted man, the second highest in the kingdom (10:3). He and Queen Esther are the leading characters of the book. From a human point of view, he is well qualified to write it, but only God knows who really did.

The setting for this historical account takes place in Persia, a large pagan empire ruled by Xerxes. Many Jews brought here during the captivity, and their descendants, have chosen to remain in the land rather than return to Jerusalem and Judah.

Esther is the only book of the Bible that does not mention the name of God. Although His name is not found here, this does not mean He is absent from all the action that takes place. He stands in the shadows. He waits in the wings—preparing, observing, and acting through His people to accomplish His purposes. He allows the pagans to do things on their own, but He will confront, restrain, and bring to a halt their actions. He remains in control through His providence—ruling, overruling.

Purim is

> a Jewish festival celebrated during the thirteen to fifteen days of the month Adar. On this occasion the Book of Esther is read, and traditionally the congregation in the synagogue shouts and boos whenever the name of Haman is mentioned. The Book of Esther gives the origin of the festival.[27]

ANALYTICAL OVERVIEW

I.   The demise of Queen Vashti (1:1–22)
II.   The selection of Esther as queen (2:1–20)
III. The discovery of Mordecai (2:21–23)
IV.   The plot of Haman (3:1–15)
V.   The reactions of Mordecai and Esther (4:1–17)
VI.   The plan of Queen Esther (5:1–14)
VII. The reward for Mordecai (6:1–14)
VIII. The request of Queen Esther (7:1–6)
IX.   The downfall of Haman (7:7–10)
X.   The edict of King Xerxes (8:1–17)
XI.   The triumph of the Jews (9:1–19)
XII. The celebration of Purim (9:20–32)
XIII. The greatness of Mordecai (10:1–3)

PRACTICAL ASPECTS

It has been said that the world has never been moved by mildly interested people. It took yearning, burning Martin Luther to bring about the Reformation. Paul, not knowing what would happen to him in Jerusalem, declares, "I do not consider my life of any account as dear to myself" (Acts 20:24 NASB). Young Queen Esther tells Mordecai that she will go into the presence of King Xerxes, "which was not according to the law, and if I perish, I perish" (4:16).

What dedication! This is far deeper than mere lip service. It is the decision of the will followed by definite action regardless of the outcome—life or death. This is the kind that gains the victor's crown. How deep is your dedication to the Lord?

What is impressive about the story of Esther and Mordecai is their togetherness in the common cause for survival. Esther is young, and her cousin Mordecai is of the older generation. A generation gap does not keep them from working hand in hand. This is the way it should be: youth working with the old, the old with the young. A union such as this has greater potential for good than each group serving its own special interests. Both make valuable contributions to one another. The old need the young to keep from drying up, and the young need the old to keep from blowing up. We need each other.

Job: Dry Your Tears

Is yours an experience like that of Job who expresses his deep hurt by saying, "My face is red with weeping, deep shadows ring my eyes" (16:16 NIV)? Or like the Psalmist, "My tears have been my food day and night" (Ps. 42:3 NIV)? Under pressure, we release tears as a relief mechanism. But they are something more than that. Tears are the diamonds of devotion, precious to God. He understands them. He loves. He cares. He knows. He remembers. He comforts. He heals. He restores. He blesses.

He does not condemn you for crying. The Man of Sorrows had tears also. But God does not want you to cry all through life. There comes a time in our spiritual development when God says, "Dry your tears. Now you must be the man."

This is what He says to Job: "Brace yourself like a man" (38:3). Face the reality of My greatness. Drop your notions. Receive My truth. I am with you to bless you. Believe Me and go on with your life.

In essence, this is what the Book of Job is all about—suffering with its unanswered questions, its humanistic reasoning and solutions, and in time, its divine revelation. All of a sudden, Job experiences indescribable sufferings. His friends attempt to comfort him but fail miserably. Elihu speaks to the men wisely. It is God Who, in His time, comes to Job in a revelation of His greatness. This becomes the turning point to better things. Job repents and is blessed.

INFORMATIONAL MATERIAL

The Book of Job is a masterpiece of Hebrew poetry. It receives its name from the principal character mentioned in it. The author of the book is not known, even though competent scholars have come to a variety of conclusions as to who actually penned it. Nor can the date of its writing be accurately established. Numerous opinions have been posited. Regardless of the lack of full knowledge in these areas, the book is in the sacred canon and divinely inspired. Some think that it is the oldest book in the Bible.

The influence of Job reaches far and wide. The prophet Ezekiel speaks highly of him, putting him into the same character category as that of Noah and Daniel (Ezekiel 14:14, 20). Certainly this indicates that Job is a man of integrity—blameless, upright, fearing God, and shunning evil (1:1).

Also, the New Testament writer says of him that he is an example of suffering and patience (James 5:10–11). Does this not suggest that James spent time in the Book of Job?
Job is an excellent book to read in time of suffering. Not only does it focus on Job but also on God Who is in control of life.

ANALYTICAL OVERVIEW

I. Prologue (1:1–2:13)
  A. Job's first test (1:1–22)
  B. Job's second test (2:1–13)

II. Dialogue (3:1–31:40)
    A. First exchange of ideas (3:1–14:22)
    B. Second exchange of ideas (15:1–21:34)
    C. Third exchange of ideas (22:1–31:40)
III. Monologue (32:1–37:24)
    A. Elihu's involvement (32:1–22)
    B. Elihu's talk (33:1–37:24)
IV. Theologue (38:1–42:6)
    A. God's first message and Job's response (38:1–40:5)
    B. God's second message and Job's response (40:6–42:6)
V. Epilogue (42:7–17)
    A. God speaks to Job's friends (42:7–9)
    B. God blesses Job abundantly (42:10–17)

Please note that the term "theologue" is not used here according to the definition found in *Webster's Collegiate Dictionary,* tenth edition, which is "a theological student or specialist." Rather, theologue comes from two Greek words, *theos* and *logos,* meaning "God speaking."

PRACTICAL ASPECTS

God does not explain to Job why he experiences suffering. There is no verbal answer from Him. An overwhelming sense of His awesome presence and power simply does what words cannot. God alone is the answer to the problems of pain and suffering. Since we cannot define or explain God, we will have to let matters that are beyond explanation rest with Him. This is the commitment of faith in the Eternal One Who makes no mistakes and does everything well. "As for God, his way is perfect" (Ps. 18:30 NIV).

A submissive spirit to our heavenly Father saves us from anxiety, frustration, and needless speculation. This is the spirit that is blessed by Him, for our Lord is more concerned about developing our character than satisfying our curiosity. It is faith, humility, confession, repentance, and worship in response to the divine presence that bring Christian fulfillment.

When God comes on the scene, He not only makes us aware of Himself but also of ourselves. We see ourselves in new light that results in a series of changes. Job is the example. The revelation produces first, a change in him (42:1–6). This is followed by a change in others, his three friends (42:7–9). Then his circumstances are changed from poverty to plenty, from misery to mercy, from blight to blessing (42:10–17).

Throughout Scripture, it is quite evident that God's people have their sufferings and sorrows, their tears and tests. Remember the words of Jesus: "In the world you have tribulation, but take courage, I have overcome the world" (John 16:33 NASB).

While holding services in Wayne, Michigan, some years ago, I heard the concerns of a young woman soloist that I have not forgotten. Before singing, she gave a word of testimony, telling of what she was experiencing. She concluded her remarks by saying, "When I see Jesus, I am going to ask Him why I had to go through all these things."

I thought, *Dear Sister, when you see Jesus, you will not even think of asking Him why. You will be so taken up with the glory of the Lord that you will have forgotten what you went through on earth.*

Yes, just one moment in heaven will be our satisfaction and consolation!

Psalms: Sing Your Song

This inspired collection of religious lyric poetry, known as the Psalter or "praise songs," has been, and continues to be, the source of comfort and encouragement for God's people everywhere. May not this be one reason why the Psalms are so widely read? Who has not turned to this book in times of tears and trials as well as those of joy and blessedness? The Psalms fit our situation like a comfortable old shoe because their message is personal and practical for everyday living.

The Psalms are used for both a prayer book and a hymn book. In it we discover examples for effective praying. There are times when we may pray the same prayer the Psalmist does. At other times, we may incorporate into our praying the elements of praise, adoration, submission, confession, petition, anticipation, and expressions of faith.

The Psalter also serves as a hymn book for temple worship. The Hebrews love to sing. Certainly they are encouraged to do so in the Psalms. Before our Lord goes to the cross, He, with His disciples, sings the Hallel (Ps. 113–118) on that memorable night as some scholars have suggested. In our times a number of contemporary choruses are based on the Psalms, making worship more meaningful. Therefore, sing your song.

INFORMATIONAL MATERIAL

David, sometimes referred to as the "sweet singer of Israel," authored many of the psalms. He himself was also a skillful musician, playing the harp in the king's palace. Music was an important part of his life as well as that of the nation. There were others who also wrote psalms: Solomon; the sons of Korah; Asaph; Herman and Ethan, both Ezrahites; and Moses. The authorship of some of the psalms is unknown; nevertheless, they are included in this sacred collection. Some psalms are especially designated to be sung with the accompaniment of musical instruments.

There is a great variety of subject matter in the Psalms. It consists of

> acrostic poems, Psalms of thanksgiving and lamentation (both individual and national), songs of trust, songs for pilgrims, hymns of penitence, prayers of the falsely accused, historical Psalms, Psalms concerning the king, prophetic Psalms; there are hymns for festivals and chants connected with the order of temple worship.[28]

This is helpful in developing a devotional life, for the Psalms tell us how we think, feel, speak, and act in God's presence. This also helps us develop the attitudes of submission, trust, praise, and joy.

There are a number of prophecies relating to Jesus Christ, given in what are called the Messianic Psalms (Ps. 2, 16, 22, 41, 45, 72, 110, 118). They speak of His incarnation, His betrayal, His rejection, His suffering, His death, His resurrection, and His exaltation. He is Lord, and in His time He shall reign as King over all the earth.

Jesus uses the statement found in Psalm 110:1 to confuse His critics (Matt. 22:41–46). On the Day of Pentecost, Peter refers to Psalm 16 as he speaks of Christ's resurrection (Acts 2:25–28). In describing the sinfulness of mankind, Paul uses truths from several Psalms (Rom. 3:10–18; with Ps. 14:1–3; 5:9; 140:3; 10:7; 36:1). The writer to the Hebrews, in chapters one and two, quotes a number of truths from the Psalms (2:7; 104:4; 45:6–7; 102:26, 27; 110:1; 8:4–6; 22:22).

The Psalms give a revelation of the awesomeness of God (139)—His omnipotence, omnipresence, and omniscience. What a great God He is! His creative genius and power are unmatched (Ps. 19, 104). Psalms is a gold mine of truth about God, His eternal Word, and man. Dig deep in it, for therein are found eternal treasures.

OUTLINE

It is not possible to give an analytical overview of the book since each Psalm is complete in itself. From a consensus of many scholars, this outline is given.

> Book I: Psalms 1–41
> Book II: Psalms 42–72
> Book III: Psalms 73–89
> Book IV: Psalms 90–106
> Book V: Psalms 107–150

PRACTICAL ASPECTS

At dusk, a little girl was walking toward the entrance of a cemetery. Approaching her was a stranger who asked a question: "Little girl, aren't you afraid to go into the cemetery? It's getting dark." Unhesitating, she replied, "No, my home is just on the other side."

On the other side of death is the Christian's eternal home. This is why David can say, "Even though I walk through the valley of the shadow of death I will fear no evil, for You are with me" (23:4a). Therefore the believer in Jesus Christ need not fear when he walks through the valley. The Lord is with him each step of the way to his heavenly home.

In figurative language, the Psalmist likens God to a parent bird: "He will cover you with his feathers, and under his wings you will find refuge" (91:4a). The Lord gave me a vivid illustration of this during my pastorate in Swanton, Ohio. The parsonage kitchen window faced the side of the church. One day I noticed that a robin was building its nest in the eaves trough. To me this seemed very unusual because robins ordinarily build their nests in trees. In time the nest had some little ones in it. On a Sunday afternoon we had a severe storm with heavy rain, thunder, and lightning. Hurrying to the kitchen window, my wife and I watched what was happening in the eaves trough as the water poured down the roof. The mother robin made herself as big as she could; stretching her wings and clamping them down on the nest, she took the full force of the water rushing against her. All during the storm, she stayed on that nest. She did not forsake her little ones. Isn't our wonderful heavenly Father like this? In the storms of life He covers us with His presence, never forsaking us. He promised: "Lo, I am with you always, even to the end of the age" (Matt. 28:20 NASB).

In the longest of the Psalms, there is this significant statement: "Your word is a lamp to my feet, and a light for my path" (119:105 NIV). The Bible is given to us as an authoritative source of light, enabling us to see what we otherwise would not see. It gives us information, instruction, and inspiration. It never gives misinformation, because it is final, absolute, inerrant, and authoritative truth.

Reading the Bible makes us spiritually intelligent. It updates our thinking. It molds our character. In fact, every area of our life will be impacted with its many precious truths.

The Bible arouses our emotions. It alerts us to dangers. It soothes our fears. It picks us up when we are down. It spurs us on when we are tempted to give up. It gives us strength when we are weak. What a blessed book is the Psalms. It is for us in our times.

Proverbs: Apply Your Learning

It is said that Billy Graham reads a chapter in Proverbs each day. What an excellent practice. For him it has yielded rich dividends. May not this be one of many reasons why the Lord enables him to communicate so effectively with all kinds of people throughout the world?

A proverb is a short, pithy saying, containing a comparison, teaching a practical moral lesson. Its condensed substance and form attract attention and stimulate thinking. Therefore, one cannot hurriedly read over it, or he will miss its meaning. In a practical sense, it could be considered a "sentence sermon." It is for the young and old alike—a family setting, stressing spiritual, ethical, and social relationships.

At the very outset of Proverbs—and continuing fifteen times throughout the book—is the important emphasis on "the fear of the Lord," a holy reverence and respect for Him and His Word. This is the beginning of knowledge and wisdom. A wise person is a God-fearing person; conversely, this is true also.

The Proverbs is a guidebook to correctness in conduct for those being enlightened by the Word of God. Indeed, Proverbs is a rich resource for living the Christian life.

INFORMATIONAL MATERIAL

According to the following analytical overview, it is quite evident that several authors are responsible for Proverbs, the principal one being Solomon, who authored some three thousand proverbs. The wisdom with which he wrote is a gift of God. The historian tells us that "Solomon's wisdom was greater than the wisdom of all the men of the East" (1 Kings 4:30a NIV). "He was wiser than any other man" (1 Kings 4:31a NIV).

Approximately 250 years after Solomon writes the proverbs, the men of King Hezekiah's reign gain access to them. They too become a part of the Book of Proverbs.

Others who contribute to the book are unknown wise individuals, Agur and King Lemuel who also cannot be precisely identified.

On a number of occasions Jesus refers to Proverbs:

> There is ample evidence that our Lord on earth loved this book. Every now and then we get an echo of its language in His own teaching; for instance, in His words about those who seek the chief seats (cf. Prov. 25:6, 7), or the parable of the wise and foolish men and their houses (cf. Prov. 14:11), or that of the rich fool (cf. Prov. 28:1). To Nicodemus He reveals the answer to the question posed by Agur the son of Jakeh (cf. Prov. 30:4 with John 3:13). And He reminds those who, like the undiscriminating 'fools' of Proverbs, do not recognize Him or His message that 'wisdom is justified of her children.' (Matt. 11:19)[29]

Several writers of the New Testament draw on truth from Proverbs: Paul (Rom. 3:15 with Prov. 1:16), James (James 4:6 with Prov. 3:34), and Peter (2 Pet. 2:22 with Prov. 26:11).

The Book of Proverbs is an authentic, inspired document, worthy of our trust.

ANALYTICAL OVERVIEW

I.   Introduction: the purpose of Proverbs (1:1–6)
II. The importance of wisdom for godly living (1:7–9:18)
III. Solomon's proverbs of wisdom (10:1–22:16)
IV. The sayings of the wise (22:17–24:22)
V.   Additional sayings of the wise (24:23–34)
VI. Solomon's proverbs recorded by Hezekiah's men (25:1–29:27)
VII. The words of Agur (30:1–33)
VIII. The words of King Lemuel (31:1–9)
IX. The qualities of an excellent wife (31:10–31)

PRACTICAL ASPECTS

A part of wisdom is to take a look at small things that are seemingly insignificant and learn some valuable lessons from them. Agur calls attention to four small creatures and tells us why they are important (30:24–28).

First, there are the ants. They are wise, agile, and extremely industrious as they prepare food during the summer for future use in the winter—"they make hay while the sun shines." To them summer is the opportunity to work. They cannot be diverted from it. They know the winter is sure to come with its bad weather, freezing temperatures, ice, sleet, and snow. Therefore, they prepare in advance for it.

From the ants, we learn the importance of preparing in advance for the future, doing what we know must be done.

There comes a time when life is over. What then? We must, in the summertime of opportunity, prepare to meet God (Heb. 9:27–28).

The second group of small creatures Agur speaks of are the conies, or rock badgers, who dwell in the rocks. Their Creator puts them in this kind of environment to protect them from danger. Should they wander off the rocks onto the grasslands, they might become easy prey for some hungry beast.

God makes the Christian for the Rock of our Salvation, Jesus Christ. Our safety is in Him. In ourselves we are not strong enough to overcome the foe, regardless of our self-improvement concepts, our self-sufficient attitudes, and our self-determined actions. Venturing away from the Rock is dangerous and will get us into trouble. Be wise; abide in Christ.

The locusts have something to tell us: act in togetherness. "They advance together in ranks." We Christians, individualistic but not independent, are to work together with other believers for Christ and His kingdom. United efforts accomplish much.

Another small animal, "equipped with adhesive pads in climbing forms,"[30] is the lizard with its amazing agility. It can move with quickness, climb trees, walk upside down on plastered ceilings, and cling to a pane of glass.[31] They keep a watchful eye on what is happening, and at the opportune moment they can run into a king's palace.

The lesson of the lizard is obvious. Christian, keep your eyes open. Jesus teaches us to "Watch and pray" (Matt. 26:41). Paul exhorts: "Be on your guard" (1 Cor. 16:13). Be ready to respond when opportunity knocks.

May God grant us the wisdom to prepare for the future, to abide in Christ the Rock of Ages, to work together with other believers, and to always be on the alert. This is utilizing our knowledge and wisdom—applying our learning.

Ecclesiastes: Ponder Your Path

Broomhall refers to Ecclesiastes as "one of the most perplexing books in the Bible"[32]; nevertheless, it is God's revelation on the futility of materialism and its philosophy, "life under the sun." Life without God does not make sense.

An important key to understanding is found in the first and last chapters of the book (1:1–2; 12:13–14). It begins with a pessimistic view of life and ends on a positive note—God. Between these two points lies the struggle for many, which is like the road of a traveler going from vanity to verity, from frustration to satisfaction. Therefore, one must ponder the path he takes in life.

While looking for meaning and significance, we need to go far beyond self-actualization and human theories. Using the word of Ecclesiastes: We must fear God and obey Him. In New Testament language, this means to trust Jesus Christ as our personal Savior and Lord; thus we will find joyful fulfillment.

INFORMATIONAL MATERIAL

The writer of this book refers to himself as the "Preacher." He does not tell us his name; from internal evidence within the book itself, however, it seems quite clear that it is Solomon. This view is not shared by everyone.

Certainly, Solomon is the son of David. He reigns as one of the kings in Jerusalem, known for his great wisdom (1:16) and his amazing accomplishments (2:4–11). Tucked throughout the book are a number of proverbs (5:2–3; 7:1–14; 10:1–11:1). This is Solomon's style of writing, which is in keeping with Proverbs.

A superficial reading of Ecclesiastes gives us the impression that the writer is so materialistically inclined that he leaves no room for God in his search for reality. He uses expressions such as "under the sun," "all is vanity," and "striving after wind," indicating humanistic thinking. It is true that throughout most of the book God seems hidden; however, he mentions God forty times, and in the grand climax stated in 12:13–14, we may be assured that He is recognized as the final Judge with the last word.

As a writer Solomon observes, examines, evaluates, draws conclusions, illustrates, and exhorts. His sharp contrasts between life and death, wisdom and foolishness, and good and evil are used effectively. He takes the seeker of truth from the pits of despair to the place of fulfillment.

ANALYTICAL OVERVIEW

I. Prologue (1:1–11)
    A. Emptiness (1:1–2)
    B. Sameness (1:3–11)
II. The quest for meaning (1:12–2:26)
    A. An attitude of determination (1:12–18)
    B. A variety of personal experiences (2:1–26)
III. The observation of life's realities (3:1–6:12)

A. Regarding the time factor (3:1–11)
B. The fact of judgment (3:12–22)
C. The variety of activities (4:1–16)
D. The folly of vain words (5:1–7)
E. The emptiness of riches (5:8–6:12)
IV. The value of wisdom (7:1–10:20)
A. Strength (7:1–22)
B. Illumination (7:23–9:12)
C. Protection (9:13–18)
D. Success (10:1–20)
V. The call to responsibility (11:1–12:8)
A. Be diligent (11:1–8)
B. Begin in youth (11:9–12:8)
VI. Epilogue (12:9–14)
A. Purpose for writing (12:9–12)
B. Fear God and obey Him (12:13)
C. God is Judge (12:14)

Practical Aspects

There is a lot more to human life than having material things. Such a statement reminds me of my boyhood days at home. At times when I became bored because there was nothing to do, or if I wanted something with a passion, I would run to my Mother and plead, "Give me this or that," whatever it was. She usually replied, "Robert, you wouldn't be satisfied if you had the world with a fence built around it." How right Mother was. There is no satisfaction in things.

Solomon, with all his rich estates, discovers this to be true. You can almost hear his sigh as he cries out, "Vanity of vanities! All is vanity" (1:2 NASB) or "Utterly meaningless!

Everything is meaningless" (NIV). Someone has aptly commented, "Soap bubble of soap bubble, all is soap bubble."

Things do not satisfy. Take, for example, a brand-new house elegantly furnished. Within a few years, the freshness of living in it wears off and it becomes an old house. That new car with its distinctive factory smell and its purring-like-a-kitten motor has to be returned to the dealer for a major adjustment. The new suit or dress will in time go to the Salvation Army or Goodwill. Things are not lasting.

Spiritual realities are eternal. They never fade, rust, deteriorate, or wear out. There is eternal freshness and beauty in the grace of God given through Jesus Christ.

Therefore ponder your path as you walk through life.

Song of Songs: Love Your Spouse

The Song of Songs is the best of songs written by King Solomon, who was loved by his Lord (2 Sam. 12:24). It presents love in its highest form—pure, sensitive, gracious. A relationship of love is what God intends for husbands and wives to enjoy.

The Genesis record declares that God created mankind in His own image, male and female (Gen. 1:27; 5:2). Jesus Himself confirms this historical fact (Matt. 19:4); therefore, the marriage relationship is ordained by God (Gen. 2:24). To think otherwise is not only erroneous but also dangerous.

The Song of Songs is a showcase of love in its purity and passion, in its integrity and intensity. The Song is the story of true love between a man and a woman within the bonds of marriage.

INFORMATIONAL MATERIAL

There have been various opinions regarding the kind of literature the Song represents. Some have thought of it in terms of a literal story, an allegory, a dramatic parable, an extended type, or an oriental love song.

I personally think of it as a literal love story of a man and woman (Solomon and the Shulamite), couched in poetic language that is highly emotional and deeply passionate.

This has been helpful to me because I struggled for many years over the meaning of the Song. It finally made sense to me when I looked at it from the standpoint of a true, pure relationship between two lovers. After all, this is the way God made us.

I discovered that, by keeping a principle of interpretation as simple as possible, the Song was opened up to me, at least in a measure. Therefore, when you study the Song, do not attempt to read into the figures of speech and its poetic language something that is not there. Let the Word speak for itself.

Having a sense of what the Song was saying, I was enabled to see the implications of it. Certainly it describes the precious and intimate relationship between Christ and His church (cf. Eph. 5:22–33).

I would make one further suggestion. In order to increase your comprehension of and appreciation for the song, read it in the New International Version.

ANALYTICAL OVERVIEW

I. Love attracting: the courtship (1:1–3:5)
    A. Interaction of love (1:1–2:7)
    B. Invitation of love (2:8–15)
    C. Decision of love (2:16–3:5)
II. Love uniting: the wedding (3:6–5:1)
    A. Love bonded (3:6–4:15)

    B. Love consummated (4:16–5:1)

III. Love maturing: the marriage relationship (5:2–8:14)

    A. Love learning (5:2–6:3)

    B. Love growing (6:4–8:14)

PRACTICAL ASPECTS

While reading the Song, which is difficult to interpret, I was reminded of the times when I was courting my wife. Indeed those were days of excitement, expectation, and joy. Now after sixty-one years of marriage, I count my companion a prized possession: "Her worth is far above jewels" (Prov. 31:10 NASB). I continue loving her.

It is one thing to be in love during courtship days but quite another to cherish and maintain that love over the years. The Song says something about cultivating love on a high level (5:2–8:14).

After the wedding, what then? Make every effort to keep love's flame alive. It will not die out as long as both husband and wife remain in a daily, close relationship with their Lord and Savior Jesus Christ. Their marriage develops and deepens.

This is not to suggest that Christian marriage will be problem free. To be realistic, there will be differences to be resolved, adjustments to be made, and values to be prioritized. Marriage is like a ship at sea. It encounters winds and storms. At times the sailing is rough. With Christ at the helm, however, sailing is *safe*. The ship will reach its port.

Love, at times, has some painful lessons for us to learn. The Song brings out this reality (5:2–6:3). The lover desires to be near his beloved, but she is insensitive to his deep feelings. Her ardor cools momentarily. Her lover withdraws. What loss she suffers. She desperately needs him and seeks him most earnestly. Shortly thereafter, both lover and his beloved come close together again. Togetherness—what a blessing!

The marriage relationship serves as a challenge and a blessing to bring out the best in each partner. The Lord uses this kind of partnership to mature us. Here are several suggestions that may help to enrich and enliven marriage as we go through the process: Be a faithful steward of what God has entrusted to you; always keep the lines of communication open; share with one another problems, pains, and hurts, as well as joys, hopes, and ambitions; demonstrate affection with deeds not only with words; fulfill your conjugal relationships with sensitivity (1 Cor. 7:3–5); let the peace of God rule in your hearts (Col. 3:15). You are under the Lordship of Christ.

It might be well for those who are gifted in family life seminars to give at least one session for husbands and wives on a careful, tasteful, tactful exposition of the Song of Songs. This remarkable book visualizes authentic love between a man and a woman, the way God intended.

Love your spouse—tenderly!

Isaiah: Heed Your Sovereign

This inspired volume is written by Isaiah, one of the greatest of the Old Testament prophets since Moses. He writes with divine authority on two vital themes: prophecy and sovereignty.

The many prophecies—concerning the Messiah, the judgments of the nations, the restoration of Israel, the tribulation, the millennial kingdom, the Second Coming, and the new order—reveal the insight God gives the prophet. All of this indicates that God has a plan by which He is working. In His time He will usher in His eternal kingdom.

Throughout the book, the Lord is given many titles, a prominent one being "the Lord Almighty" (NIV). This puts emphasis on divine sovereignty. Every individual and all nations are accountable to Him and will ultimately answer to Him. God reigns forever!

The evident thought of Isaiah is on judgment followed by blessing. Truly, this is an exciting book to read and study. It will challenge and comfort, search and stir, thrill and threaten you.

Informational Material

The name Isaiah means "Yahweh is salvation." His ministry, covering over fifty years, has great depth and breadth. Endowed by the Spirit of the Lord, Isaiah is a gifted writer, a spiritual and social reformer, a fearless and compassionate preacher of righteousness, and a keen and foresighted statesman.

He does not minister from an ivory tower but in a real world of crisis and change. He knows his world well and is aware of the kingdom that is to come in God's time. Moreover, he knows his Lord: the Almighty and the Holy One of Israel. He is given a vision of the King.

Isaiah writes out of an environment very similar to that of our computer, space-age society. He is not shielded from the raw realities of a decadent, stubborn, permissive, yet religious generation. He participates with mankind in his struggles, hurts, and agony, yet not with his sins. He knows what real life is all about, that it is difficult, tough, and at times heartbreaking.

What about his times? He lives during the reigns of four kings: Uzziah, Jotham, Ahaz, and Hezekiah (Isa. 1:1; 2 Kings 16–20; 2 Chron. 26–32). During his time economic prosperity leads to pride and idolatry. The shrine of riches becomes a god. Isaiah is here.

In his day there is a vast military buildup. King Uzziah has an elite army of 307,500 soldiers. There are wars, tears, and suffering. Isaiah is here.

Isaiah is a witness of the decline of religion and the emergence of superficial piety. People continue going to the temple, offering sacrifices, and observing religious rituals, but they live hypocritical lives. They are role-players.

They "fear the Lord, they also served their idols" (2 Kings 17:41 NASB). Isaiah is here.

The prophet also knows something of the joy that comes when people return to the Lord. During the reign of King Hezekiah, the Passover is celebrated, resulting in "great joy" (2 Chron. 30:26).

Such are Isaiah's times—days of joy and pain, hurting and healing, victory and defeat.

ANALYTICAL OVERVIEW

I. The condemnation of sin and its judgments (1–35)
   A. The indictment against Judah and Jerusalem (1–5)
   B. The life and ministry of Isaiah (6–8)
   C. The judgment of sin and the coming of Messiah (9–12)
   D. The judgments of foreign nations (13–23)
   E. The judgments of earth and the blessings of God's grace (24–27)
   F. The six woes of warning (28–35)
II. Historical interlude (36–39)
   A. Hezekiah and the Assyrian invasion (36–37)
   B. Hezekiah's sickness and healing (38)
   C. Hezekiah and the Babylonians (39)
III. The consolation of salvation and its blessings (40–66)
   A. The greatness of God (40–48)
   B. The grace of God (49–57)
   C. The glory of God (58–66)

PRACTICAL ASPECTS

Isaiah's vision of the Lord in His glory completely transforms him. He is never again the same, cleansed from sin and called into God's service. Before this he had not seen his true self or sensed the deep spiritual need in his own heart. His face-to-face encounter with God changes all this. Does this not suggest that we will never know what we really are until we have the courage to see ourselves in God's light?

The prophet wields the sharp sword of truth, but it is bathed in oil. The sword that cuts, heals. In his thunderous denunciation of sin, he graciously and tenderly extends the invitation to come to the Lord (1:18; 55:1–3). Regardless of how great a sinner a man may be, he is invited to come. Let preachers of the gospel denounce sin, but let them always give the invitation to sinners: "Come to Christ."

Isaiah is an ardent student of the Scriptures available to him, even though at this time, the Old Testament had not been completed. Here are several examples of his knowledge of Scripture: He acknowledges and authenticates the fact that Noah was a real historical person and that the flood actually occurred (Isa. 54:9; Gen. 9:8a, 11); he proves that Sodom and Gomorrah were actual cities (Isa. 13:19; Gen. 19:24); he recognizes that the drying up of the sea was true (Isa. 51:10; Exod. 14:21–22); he writes of David's victory at Perazim (Isa. 28:21; 2 Sam. 5:20). We can rely on the authenticity of the Old Testament.

This book contains a wide range of subjects. We will be the wiser for reading it. It interlocks with both Old and New Testaments. It confirms Old Testament history and is a basis for New Testament theology. Isaiah bonds both testaments into one divine revelation from God.

The busy prophet is deeply involved in the Lord's service, yet he is not too occupied to pray. Throughout his book, you will discover a number of prayers. Look for them. Jesus teaches that men ought always to pray (Luke 18:1).

Isaiah is the book to be read for our times. There is a striking similarity between Isaiah's day and ours. When we look at the sins of our society, they seem to be an exact duplication of what was said of the prophet's generation. Mr. Average American may be a churchgoer; but, alas, his lifestyle contradicts his religious profession. Isaiah witnesses a similar situation.

Sin has a hardening effect upon the human heart. The greater the sin, the harder the heart. Isaiah does not allow this to happen to him. He remains sensitive and compassionate. He is not overwhelmed by the hypocrisy and abominable vices he witnesses daily. He keeps focused on his Lord. This is the secret of the overcomer: "Looking unto Jesus."

Reading Isaiah once is not enough. Spend time in the book. It will put strength in your soul, warmth in your heart, and drive in your holy ambition. Heed your Sovereign.

Jeremiah: Continue Your Praying

Here is a book written by a priest's son. In our day, we would call him a PK (preacher's kid). Jeremiah is blessed with a religious heritage. From the small town of his birth, Anathoth, he goes to the city of Jerusalem in response to the call of God and becomes His spokesman to the entire nation. What a ministry Jeremiah has!

This prophet lives during the declining days of the kingdom. His society continues its downward course away from God. Morals are collapsing. Idolatry is advancing. Sin is abounding. Leaders in both the political and religious realms are leading the nation step by step to its destruction.

The Sovereign God is very much aware of this; therefore, He calls Jeremiah to proclaim His message, to stem the tide of wickedness, and to call the people back to Himself. In this book the prophet points out the abominable sins of society, those of forsaking the Lord and of worshiping idols. Unless there is repentance, the inevitable will come to pass—the destruction of the nation. Jeremiah tells us that the Babylonians capture Jerusalem and the nation is reduced to shambles.

Informational Material

For nearly half a century Jeremiah carries out his ministry faithfully, beginning at an early age in youth when the Lord appointed him to be a prophet to the closing days of his life in Egypt. He leaves us with a rich heritage of truth, forged on the anvil of obedience, being hammered by the pressures of his times.

In addition to the work of Jeremiah, there are other prophets the Lord uses in making known His word. God also calls Zephaniah and Habakkuk to witness against their unbelieving generation. God speaks clearly to the idolatrous people, longing to lead them to repentance and restoration.

For twenty-three years, Jeremiah preaches without success. The crowds do not take him seriously. They feel secure in their false refuge of unbelief. They think that the marching armies of the Babylonians cannot overtake their capital city, Jerusalem. Is not the temple here? Need we worry? Consequently, they do not listen to the prophet (25:3).

In fact, they harden their hearts and verbally abuse and persecute him. Even the people of his hometown seek to take his life (11:21). Others slander him (18:18). Pashhur the priest has him beaten and put in stocks (20:2). Priests, prophets, and people demand his death (26:8). The wicked King Jehoiakim cuts up his scroll and orders it burned (36:23). Accused of being unpatriotic, Jeremiah is arrested, beaten, and put in prison (37:11–16). Officials of King Zedekiah have him placed in a cistern where he sinks in the mud (38:6). Finally his dwelling place is the guardhouse (38:28).

This is what Jeremiah goes through in order to be true to his Lord. He does not endure all this because of his own strength and determination. God promised him at the very beginning, "They will fight against you but will not over-come you, for I am with you and will rescue you" (1:19 NIV). Jeremiah's life and ministry are a testimony to God's power and faithfulness.

This book will prove to be a great encouragement to all who suffer for the gospel's sake.

ANALYTICAL OVERVIEW

I. Jeremiah is appointed a prophet (1:1–19)
   A. His call (1:1–16)
   B. His purpose (1:17–19)
II. Jeremiah speaks to the nation (2:1–20:18)
   A. About sin and the coming judgment (2:1–12:17)
   B. About the certainty and intensity of judgment (13:1–20:18)
III. Jeremiah speaks to leaders and people (21:1–25:38)
   A. The word for kings (21:1–22:30)
   B. The word for shepherds and prophets (23:1–40)
   C. The word for the people (24:1–25:38)
IV. Jeremiah encounters opposition (26:1–29:32)
   A. Threats from leaders and people (26:1–24)
   B. Conflicts with false prophets (27:1–29:32)
V. Jeremiah prophesies about the restoration (30:1–33:26)
   A. Based on divine authority (30:1–31:40)
   B. Proved by his purchase of land (32:1–33:26)
VI. Jeremiah urges obedience to God's Word (34:1–35:19)
   A. An example of disobedience (34:1–22)
   B. An example of obedience (35:1–19)
VII. Jeremiah ministers under restrictions (36:1–32)
   A. Dictates the word to Baruch (36:1–10)
   B. Learns the word is destroyed (36:11–26)

C. Prepares another scroll (36:27–32)

VIII. Jeremiah witnesses the siege and captivity (37:1–45:5)

A. Beaten and imprisoned (37:1–38:28)

B. Treated kindly by the Babylonians (39:1–40:16)

C. Forced to go to Egypt (41:1–44:30)

D. Encouraged Baruch (45:1–5)

IX. Jeremiah prophesies about foreign nations (46:1–51:64)

A. Egypt (46:1–28)

B. The Philistines (47:1–7)

C. Moab (48:1–47)

D. Ammon, Edom, Damascus, Kedar, Hazor, Elam (49:1–39)

E. Babylon (50:1–51:64)

X. Appendix: historical information (52:1–34)

PRACTICAL ASPECTS

Like so many other prophetic writings, Jeremiah tells of the sovereign power of God. He is the Almighty. He controls the destiny of nations. No civilization can last long without Him. He may be neglected and rejected, but He will have the final word in dealing with mankind. Therefore, we dare not limit Him, box Him in, keep Him quiet, hold Him down, or shut Him out. All such attempted actions are in vain.

Great personalities, mighty armies, and strong nations have tried to do this but failed miserably. In His time and way, the everlasting God accomplishes His work—invades, captures, takes over, and reigns. Ask the people of Jeremiah's day.

Jeremiah does the work of an evangelist and models this ministry well. With truth blazing in his heart, he preaches as "dying man to dying man." In his strong and vehement denunciations of sin and threats of the coming judgment, he is compassionate. He weeps inwardly and unashamedly. Listen to his cry, "Oh, my anguish, my anguish! I writhe in pain. Oh, the agony of my heart!" (4:19 NIV). "But if you do not listen, I will weep in secret because of your pride; my eyes will weep bitterly, overflowing with tears, because the Lord's flock will be taken captive" (13:17 NIV).

Perhaps we should ask ourselves this heart-searching question: Do we weep over the condition of the lost who are on their way to eternal damnation? Do we really care about them? It might be that our culture has such a hardening effect upon us that we have lost our tears of compassion. May God give us tender hearts in a hard-hearted society. Jeremiah is our example as is our Savior Jesus Christ.

Jeremiah's service, tears, compassion, sincerity, and loyalty are the result of God's work in his life, equipping him to do His will. (Review chapter one.) The prophet always stays close to his Lord; he is a praying man.

When you read his book carefully, you will notice that many of his words are his prayers. He pours out his heart to God constantly. This speaks loudly of the fact that the Word of God was written in a spirit of prayer.

Jeremiah teaches us that praying helps us over the hard places in life. In prayer we receive strength from our Lord to carry on; therefore, continue your praying.

Lamentations:
Contemplate Your End

The Book of Lamentations is an integral part of the divine revelation. Its disclosure of the terrible consequences of sin cuts across the grain of popular opinion. We do not want to think of judgment and death, especially if we are young and healthy. A wise and intelligent person will give these important matters serious consideration and act accordingly.

Is it not true that our perspective on life is slanted in the wrong direction? We think of enjoying ourselves with all the gusto and hype we possibly can. After all, we go this way only once and then who cares after that?

The answer is, we had better care. This is why God in His mercy gives us Lamentations, that we may think in advance of our end. Contemplate it seriously. This historical record tells us honestly what happens to a people, a nation that persists in sinning. Putting it bluntly, they suffer the consequences.

For years the Lord deals faithfully with Judah and Jerusalem, but His loving entreaties are brushed aside. Jeremiah weeps as he tells them of the coming judgment. His message is rejected. The day comes when the Babylonians capture and destroy Jerusalem. Lamentations tells us of the sorrow and agony that follows. Alas, the people do not contemplate their end.

INFORMATIONAL MATERIAL

It is quite evident that Jeremiah authors this book even though the critics might question it. Jeremiah witnesses the decline and fall of the kingdom, being an eyewitness to all that is happening and knowing of the sufferings that follow. He himself experiences indescribable pain. He hurts deeply. He goes into detail to describe the sufferings.

In the Hebrew Bible this book is called "How," translated from the first word of the text. Lamentations is located in the Hagiographa of the Jewish Scriptures. In our Bibles it follows Jeremiah. Its location in the Bible does not in any way affect its authenticity and canonicity.

The expressions "daughter of Jerusalem" or "daughter of Zion" refer to the people of the city. In personifying Jerusalem, Jeremiah speaks of it as a widow who weeps (1:1–2).

Archer notes "that the first four chapters are written in the acrostic form. Chapters one, two, and four are therefore twenty-two verses long, each verse beginning with the successive letter of the Hebrew alphabet. Chapter three, however, contains sixty-six verses, since three successive verses are allotted to each letter of the alphabet."[33]

ANALYTICAL OVERVIEW

I. The desolation of Jerusalem (1:1–22)
   A. The city mourns (1:1–11)

B. The Lord punishes (1:12–19)
C. The afflicted prays (1:20–22)
II. The anger of the Lord (2:1–22)
    A. Against the city (2:1–9)
    B. Against the people (2:10–17)
    C. The call to prayer (2:18–22)
III. The witness of Jeremiah (3:1–66)
    A. God's sovereignty (3:1–18)
    B. God's love (3:19–39)
    C. God's actions (3:40–54)
    D. God's help (3:55–66)
IV. The severity of judgment (4:1–22)
    A. Drastic changes experienced (4:1–12)
    B. Spiritual leaders judged (4:13–20)
    C. Edom to be punished (4:21–22)
V. The prayer of Jeremiah (5:1–22)
    A. The confession of sin (5:1–18)
    B. The request for restoration (5:19–22)

PRACTICAL ASPECTS

One of the sins of society in Jeremiah's day, leading to the downfall of the nation, is that of indifference: "She did not consider her future" (1:9 NIV). An unknown poet's perspective is thought provoking:

What Then?
When the plants of our mighty cities
Have turned out their last finished work;
When our merchants have sold their last yardage
And have dismissed the last tired clerk;
When our banks have raked in their last dollar

145

And paid out their last dividend;
When the Judge of the earth says, "Closed for the night,"
And asks for a balance—what then?

When the choir has sung its last anthem,
And the preacher has made his last prayer;
When the people have heard their last sermon,
And the sound has died out on the air;
When the Bible lies closed on the altar,
And the pews are all empty of men,
And each one stands facing his record,
And the Great Book is opened—what then?

When the actors have played their last drama,
And the mimic has made his last pun;
When the film has flashed its last picture,
And the scoreboard displayed its last run;
When the crowds seeking pleasure have vanished
And gone out in the darkness again;
When the Trumpet of the Ages has sounded,
And we stand up before Him—what then?

When the bugle's call sinks into silence,
And the long-marching columns stand still;
When the captain has given his last orders,
And they've captured the last fort and hill,
And the flag has been hauled in from the masthead,
And the wounded afield have checked in,
And a world that rejected its Savior,
Is asked for a reason—what then?

—Anonymous

Ezekiel: Know Your God

"God strengthens" is the meaning of Ezekiel's name. How appropriate it is, for God truly strengthens the prophet to stand up to those who are obstinate and to carry out His ministry. The mindset of the people is against the Lord. Their waywardness destroys their sensitivity to Him. They need to know Who He is.

Ezekiel is a visible sign for prophetic statements. He carries out significant acts to illustrate his messages. For example, he uses a brick or clay tablet and other materials to represent the siege of Jerusalem (4:1–17). In another instance, he prepares baggage to go away to impress upon those who watch him of the reality of the Exile (12:1–28).

We may liken Ezekiel to a television screen in Babylon. The captives who are there get their news from Jerusalem by watching and hearing him. The Lord reveals in visions what is happening in the homeland: the sinful lifestyle of the temple worshipers (8:1–11:25); the rebellion of Zedekiah (17:1–24); and the day the king of Babylon lays siege to Jerusalem (24:1–27).

This book provides us with a partial picture of life during the Exile. It holds out the hope of a new order; hence, the themes of deportation and restoration are emphasized. Ezekiel gives us the negatives and positives of divine truth.

INFORMATIONAL MATERIAL

While living in Jerusalem, Ezekiel is profoundly impressed by Jeremiah, who continues ministering until and after the capture of the city. Jeremiah remains but Ezekiel is taken to Babylon where Daniel resides. Several years before, Daniel had become a hostage of King Nebuchadnezzar.

The Sovereign Lord raises up three men—Jeremiah, Daniel, and Ezekiel—to be His spokesmen. He strategically locates them during the days of divine judgments. Jeremiah is God's servant in Judah, suggesting that grace walks hand in hand with judgment. How good God is.

Daniel is God's statesman in the king's court, while Ezekiel is God's prophet to the captives. Ezekiel is "among the exiles" (1:1), yet the hand of the Lord is upon him (1:3). He is given a ministry in this kind of environment for approximately twenty-two years.

The influence of Daniel is so outstanding that Ezekiel mentions his name three times (14:14, 20; 28:3). He is known as a righteous man.

Ezekiel is a prophet. The prophetic office is of a twofold nature: namely, that of forthtelling God's message of "thus says the Sovereign Lord"; and that of foretelling, declaring in advance what is going to take place. Ezekiel carries out both functions.

As a writer, he uses a variety of literary devices to package the message, such as visual signs, parables, riddles, proverbs, allegories, symbols, and lamentations. Truth put in these various forms attracts attention, arouses interest, and aids memory.

The content of his book is put in chronological order (8:1; 20:1; 24:1; 29:1, 17; 30:20; 31:1; 32:1, 17; 33:21; 40:1). This indicates that Ezekiel is a well-organized writer. Many of his expressions are used by John in the Book of Revelation.

ANALYTICAL OVERVIEW

I. The call of Ezekiel (1:1–3:27)
    A. The vision of glory (1:1–28)
    B. The work of the Spirit (2:1–10)
    C. The authority of the Word (3:1–27)
II. The sin and judgment of the house of Israel (4:1–24:27)
    A. Prophecies of the fall of Jerusalem (4:1–7:27)
    B. Visions of abominations in the temple (8:1–11:25)
    C. The certainty of the exile (12:1–24:27)
III. The sin and judgment of pagan nations (25:1–32:32)
    A. Prophecies concerning Israel's neighbors (25:1–17)
    B. Prophecies concerning Tyre and Sidon (26:1–28:26)
    C. Prophecies concerning Egypt (29:1–32:32)
IV. The desolation and restoration of Israel (33:1–39:29)
    A. Prophecies of judgments and blessings (33:1–36:38)
    B. Prophecies of victory and glory (37:1–39:29)
V. The vision of the new order (40:1–48:35)
    A. The new temple (40:1–47:12)
    B. The land inherited (47:13–48:35)

PRACTICAL ASPECTS

In the example of Ezekiel, we observe that God always knows where to place His people, whether it be behind an iron curtain, a bamboo curtain, or a secular curtain. They will be loving Him and serving Him. You will find them in cities, the country, churches, factories, colleges, offices, hospitals, and government agencies. The list is endless. God has His people everywhere. His great family reaches around the world.

Whenever the Sovereign God chooses to shake, shape, or shock society, He raises up individuals to do His will. Ezekiel is no exception. He is God's man for the appointed place at the right time.

The person God calls is supernaturally equipped to carry out His purposes. Ezekiel is such an individual. God touches him, lays His hand upon him (1:3), testing him with difficult circumstances and assignments. He teaches him total dependence upon the Word and the Spirit.

The task for which we are responsible is not "a piece of cake." Ask Ezekiel. The people to whom he ministers are the kind we would think are beyond help. They are hard of heart, defiant emotionally because of the Lord's discipline, and rebellious, unsure of their future in a pagan land.

Serving God is not a Sunday school picnic, a march in a dress parade, nor a hero's welcome after some great achievement. Put yourself in Ezekiel's place. How do you respond to difficult, sometimes impossible, situations?

Circumstances and environment do not make the man or woman—making the proper response to circumstances by contact with heaven, does. Ezekiel is among the exiles in a foreign country; Moses is forty years in a burning desert; Paul, in a Roman prison; Jeremiah, in a decadent society. Yet all of them have a dynamic ministry.

It does not take an ideal environment to produce an effective Christian. God makes His kind of person through a variety of circumstances. He molds Ezekiel. He makes us what He wants us to be if we wholeheartedly yield to Him.

Daniel: Continue Your Witness

This book is packed with exciting truths revealing the development of human history from the time of the Babylonian Empire to the Second Coming of Christ, the climactic point of the ages. It is written by a man of God, Daniel, who holds important positions in pagan governments for approximately seventy-some years, from youth to old age, living away from his beloved homeland.

This is an important book to study because it is an infallible source of biblical prophecy, an encouragement to put our faith in God's authentic Word, and an incentive to be on the alert for signs of, and trends toward, Christ's coming. Moreover, it brightens our hope and deepens our love for Christ and His coming kingdom.

If we know the content of Daniel and observe from whence history has come and where it is going, we will have insight into God's sovereign workings.

Daniel's noble example of consistency and commitment to his Lord is the clarion call to continue our witness wherever we are placed in the providence of God—be it at home among loved ones and friends or in a strange land where pagan lifestyles are practiced.

Informational Material

The Book of Daniel has the unqualified endorsement of Jesus Christ, who calls attention to it in the Olivet discourse: "Therefore when you see the ABOMINATION OF DESOLATION which was spoken of through Daniel the prophet, standing in the holy place (let the reader understand)" (Matt. 24:15 NASB). Christ Himself calls Daniel a prophet and validates his message.

The basic theme of the book has to do with the sovereignty of God in dealing with pagan nations, exercising sovereign power over them and over His own people, the Jews, who have been exiled from their country and taken captive by Babylon.

Daniel lives in times of traumatic change, overwhelming and heartbreaking. No doubt he is among the first of the captives taken from Jerusalem to Babylon to live in this foreign land for the rest of his life, away from loved ones, friends, and his native country.

Since Jeremiah ministers for many years in and around Jerusalem, without doubt Daniel is influenced by him and perhaps is brought to faith in the Lord through his ministry. During this period as Daniel is brought to the fore in government circles in Babylon, the prophet Ezekiel is raised up by God to speak to the Jews, the many captives taken from Judah and Jerusalem.

Daniel lives throughout the entire period of captivity, from his youth under Nebuchadnezzar (605 B.C.) to Cyrus the Persian (536 B.C.). If he were fifteen or nineteen years of age when he went to Babylon, he would be eighty-five or eighty-nine when he writes the book. Thus this book of prophecy is written by a man of maturity, deeply devoted to his God, in times of the misery being experienced by the nation of Israel. Yet God has not completely forsaken His people because He has appointed Jeremiah, Daniel, and Ezekiel as His spokesmen to them.

The Book of Daniel is apocalyptic literature; that is, future events are revealed through symbols, pointing to realities. Truth is communicated by pictures rather than by definitions. This kind of literature employs numbers, color, and sound. It makes much of vision and presents the coming Messiah who will set up His kingdom. It is used as a means of encouragement for the people of God.

When the seventy years of captivity end, Daniel remains in Babylon (12:13). There is no record of his returning to Jerusalem.

ANALYTICAL OVERVIEW

I. The sovereignty of God in history (1:1–6:28)
    A. Daniel in Babylon (1:1–21)
    B. The dream of Nebuchadnezzar (2:1–49)
    C. The fiery furnace (3:1–30)
    D. The great tree (4:1–37)
    E. The feast of Belshazzar (5:1–31)
    F. The den of lions (6:1–28)

II. The sovereignty of God in prophecy (7:1–12:13)
    A. The four great beasts (7:1–28)
    B. The ram and the goat (8:1–27)
    C. The prayer of Daniel and God's answer (9:1–27)
    D. The vision of a heavenly being (10:1–21)
    E. The conflicts of the kings (11:1–45)
    F. The activities of the end times (12:1–13)

Practical Aspects

The Book of Daniel is a revelation of the power of God to care for His own and keep them in the midst of a hostile, aggressive environment of paganism. The Lord preserves His witness, Daniel, for many years.

We live in a world that is not a friend to grace. Our children know this as they experience the breakup of the home. Our young people know it as they rub shoulders with a worldly crowd given to sex, drugs, violence, and defiance. Those who are part of the workforce, whether in the office or factory, are daily bombarded with profanity and enticements to immorality. Nevertheless, by the power of God, we may be kept throughout our entire lifetime. Remember Daniel.

As Daniel is supernaturally enlightened with respect to the course that history would take, he warns us that pagan kingdoms come to an end. He cites specifically Babylon, Medo-Persia, Greece, Rome, and the empire at the time of the end—all are destined for destruction. Mankind's feeble attempt to govern himself is a failure. In God's time, human government will be superseded by the regal, righteous reign of Jesus Christ.

This is God's gracious promise and the believer's blessed hope. Jesus Christ is destined for the throne over all the earth. We call this the millennial reign, or as John puts it in the Revelation, the thousand-years' reign.

Daniel's life is an example for praying. He began while young to call on the Lord, continuing his praying to the very end. He is not too busy, because of his governmental responsibilities, to pray.

Let us tiptoe our way into his prayer chamber and listen to him as he pours out his heart to God. This puts us on holy ground, making us aware of the Lord's awesome presence. Read prayerfully Daniel 9:1–27 and note that while he is speaking, the Lord answers him and dispatches Gabriel to instruct him.

This biblical truth is valid: God answers prayer. He has a variety of ways to respond to our heart cries; therefore, do not allow your thoughts to determine how God will respond to you. He answers our prayers according to His sovereign will and way.

Hosea: Express Your Love

A mother's heart was broken because of her wayward daughter. How she longed to have her home. She did her best in searching for her but without success.

One day she was told by a friend where the young woman might be living. The mother had a large picture made of herself with words written underneath it, "I love you always," and had it placed where she thought her daughter might be.

Day after day, crowds gathered around the picture and wondered at the meaning of it. Sometime later, the young woman noticed the crowd nearby and went over to see what was happening.

It was a picture of her mother, who still loved her regardless of what she had done. Overwhelmed with this assurance of love, she hurried home to be received with wide-open arms.

Is not this a perfect illustration of God's love for us? The Lord tells us that He loves us and wants us for Himself.

This is the story of Hosea loving his prodigal wife—loving her always. Actually the book of the prophet Hosea is the truth of John 3:16 in action during the Old Testament dispensation.

INFORMATIONAL MATERIAL

The name of Hosea means "help," "deliverance," "salvation." The content of his book is perhaps a general summary of the leading thoughts contained in his public addresses. They are excerpts from sermons delivered over a number of years.

Hosea ministers in days of religious apostasy. The worship of Jehovah and the idolatrous religion of Baal are mixed together, retaining the Lord's name but following a ritual taken from the corrupt practices of Baal worship. The God of Israel is placed on an equality with the gods of the heathen; consequently, morals collapse and human corruption abounds. Here is a merger of the sacred with the secular.

As if this seamy side of life is not enough, the prophet has his heart broken by an unfaithful wife. Yet the Lord does not forsake him. Through these tragic experiences, God transforms his inner life, enlarging him, enriching him, and enabling him to love and preach as no other man. His Christlike compassion moves him to confront Israel forthrightly and lovingly, and save the wicked nation from the dreadful doom into which it was about to plunge. Indeed, this book is but little more than "a succession of sobs."

Hosea, like other biblical writers, is a man of the Word. It is quite evident that he searches the Old Testament Scriptures that are available to him in his times. He establishes the historicity of both people and places (Hos. 9:9–10; 12:3; Num. 25:3; Judg. 19; Gen. 25:26).

ANALYTICAL OVERVIEW

I. The preparation of the prophet for ministry (1:1–3:5)
   A. The pain of a marital relationship (1:1–2:1)

PRACTICAL ASPECTS

God always prepares His man for His service. A call to service is a call to preparation. For years, Hosea is in the process of being prepared—trained to carry out the will of God. That preparation is not in a formal educational system of higher learning but rather in the common experiences of everyday life through agony, heartbreak, and suffering. The man of God, before he speaks the Word of God, learns to love as God loves. With a heart filled and flooded with divine love, Hosea speaks to the nation. His fiery denunciations of sin are communicated in a spirit of brokenness and compassion. God hurts Hosea deeply to make him healing balm for wicked, wounded Israel. This is what makes Hosea Godlike.

In Hosea the Lord wants Israel to know that He cares for His wayward people: "I cared for you in the wilderness" (13:5 NASB). They are the objects of His love. They are important to Him. He creates them. He wants them for Himself. He has plans for them.

Hosea unveils truths of sin, of judgment, and of love.

> In these pages we have first a revelation of what sin is at its deepest and its worst; secondly, we have a revelation of the nature of judgment, and of its inevitable activity

as the result of sin; and finally, we have a revelation of the unconquerable force of love. . . . Sin against love is the most heinous sin of all. . . . the deepest and most awful thing in the realm of sin is that of doing despite to love.[34]

Inevitably, sin brings its losses to those who embrace it: the loss of things (2:9). The idolatrous person experiences loss, the loss of worth (2:10). Israel feels cheap, worthless— the loss of a healthy self-image. Sin makes people feel like tramps. Sin robs us, throws us down mercilessly. It hurts us. It separates us from God.

The marvel of the message of Hosea is that God cares about us. The book closes with an invitation to undeserving people: return to the Lord who loves you (14:1–9).

Joel: Update Your Worldview

In clear and concise language, Joel reveals truth that has been given to him through a divine revelation about "the day of the Lord." Five times this expression is used in his prophecy (1:15; 2:1, 11, 31; 3:14), indicating that it has historical and eschatological significance. Joel tells us that what happens in history regarding God's judgments, such as the plague of locusts, prefigures the final day of the Lord. This ultimately yields a pattern appropriate for the following generations unto the end of time.

The pattern observable is judgment, the call to repentance, followed by forgiveness and blessing. These timeless truths serve as principles by which God governs. This biblical revelation is the basis for thinking in terms of a worldview. What happened in history will take place in the future, even in the end time.

Therefore, in order to have a proper worldview and keep it updated, we must always take God into consideration. It is not enough to look only at the manward, materialistic side of life; we must also see it from God's perspective, without which our view will not only be limited but also greatly distorted and therefore erroneous.

The Book of Joel updates our worldview.

INFORMATIONAL MATERIAL

Nothing is known about the author of this book, except that he is the son of Pethuel (1:1); nor do we know when Joel pens his prophecy. A number of scholars have suggested the date of 830 B.C.; the liberal critics date it much later. There is greater support for the early date from conservative scholars.

> Joel's book has been described as a literary gem which highlights his writing ability and his purity of style. He carefully polishes and beautifies his work as perhaps no other Old Testament writer does. The language is forceful and the description of the locust invasion minutely accurate. He employs a historical incident to foretell the coming judgment of God against Judah, and from there he goes on to the judgments of the "day of the Lord" which are still future.[35]

This book also predicts the outpouring of the Spirit that is fulfilled on the day of Pentecost (2:28–32), being witnessed by Peter and the early followers of Christ (Acts 2). In this prophecy Joel gives us a glimpse of the church age, from Pentecost to the Millennium.

Another remarkable prophecy to be fulfilled in eschatological times is that of water flowing from the house of God in Jerusalem (3:18). This concept is also stated by Ezekiel (47:1–5) and Zechariah (14:8), both of whom come years after Joel. This occurs during the "day of the Lord."

"The day of the Lord" does not refer to one twenty-four hour period, a week, or a year, but to a determined portion of time in which God does His work, whether in judgment or blessing.

ANALYTICAL OVERVIEW

I. Superscription (1:1)
II. The historical Day of the Lord (1:2–20)
    A. A description of the locust plague (1:2–12)
    B. A call to repentance (1:13–20)
III. The typical Day of the Lord (2:1–27)
    A. A picture of God's wrath (2:1–11)
    B. A call to repentance (2:12–18)
    C. A response from God promising blessing (2:19–27)
IV. The eschatological Day of the Lord (2:28–3:21)
    A. The outpouring of the Spirit (2:28–32)
    B. The judgment of God upon the nations (3:1–17)
    C. The blessings of the new order (3:18–21)

PRACTICAL ASPECTS

The Book of Joel tells us where human history is going and how it will end. It gives us an awareness of the awesomeness of God in carrying out His administrative processes according to certain principles, practices, and patterns.

The Lord is not far off from us, disinterested, or unconcerned about what is going on in our lives. He truly cares about us and for us. In fact, He is vitally involved with us, even though we give this little thought most of the time.

Therefore, God has to use drastic measures such as He uses in Joel's day to awaken us to reality that we might draw close to Him, for He desires us for Himself. His sovereign acts are intended for our good and His glory.

Since our God is in charge of all things, is it not wise to yield ourselves to His Lordship?

Amos: Consider Your Future

A thundering voice is heard in Israel. It is that of the Lord Who roars from Zion through a plainclothes prophet named Amos, a shepherd and a caretaker of sycamore fig trees. Without a formal education in the school of the prophets, he is selected by God to be His spokesman to the people of the northern kingdom—Israel.

Actually, Amos is a resident of the southern kingdom, Judah, but he is sent north to proclaim "thus saith the Lord." How wise is God in His dealings with people. For years He has Amos in preparation for this ministry. Having lived in the out-of-doors, strong and healthy with an objective point of view, he boldly declares the message untainted by compromise or favoritism. He is fearless in his exposé of sin, warning of the consequences of living wickedly. Unless the nation seeks God, it will go into exile.

Amos says:

Look at your sinful life. It displeases and grieves God. It demands and deserves His righteous judgment. Doom awaits you. You will go into captivity. Consider your future and turn to the Lord before the dreadful day of reckoning.

This is the "sharp teeth" message of the Book of Amos.

Informational Material

Amos lives in days of peace and prosperity. This in time leads to unwarranted freedoms, luxury, and ease—ultimately resulting in moral and social decay. A message from God is desperately needed and Amos is called to deliver it.

Those to whom he ministers are far from God. A spirit of indifference and self-indulgence grips them. Material gain is their driving passion. The merchants are deceitful; the judges, dishonest. The poor suffer because of the oppression of the rich.

Surprisingly, the people are outwardly religious. Their elaborate ceremonies and religious observances are devoted largely to false gods. Here is a nation of religious sinners.

Amos comes to this people, who feel no need for his kind of preaching, which is blunt, direct, courageous, and dynamic. Only his message from God can save the nation from ruin, but it is not received. Sometime later, Israel goes into exile, being captured by the Assyrians.

Certainly, Amos is a wise and gifted preacher. He knows how to gain the attention of the people. His first approach to them is considered a psychological classic. His style has literary merit, making excellent use of metaphors, sarcasm, similes, eloquent expressions, and poetry of high quality.[36] His message is powerful and passionate, for he is a preacher of righteousness and truth in keeping with the teachings of the Pentateuch.

ANALYTICAL OVERVIEW

I. Superscription (1:1–2)
    A. The writer: Amos (1:1)
    B. The word of the Lord (1:2)
II. The transgressions and punishments of nations (1:3–2:16)
    A. Damascus (1:3–5)
    B. Gaza (1:6–8)
    C. Tyre (1:9–10)
    D. Edom (1:11–12)
    E. Ammon (1:13–15)
    F. Moab (2:1–3)
    G. Judah (2:4–5)
    H. Israel (2:6–16)
III. The word of the Lord to Israel (3:1–6:14)
    A. God's determination to punish Israel (3:1–15)
    B. God's gracious dealings with Israel (4:1–13)
    C. God's kindness and severity toward Israel (5:1–6:14)
IV. The five visions of Amos (7:1–9:10)
    A. The locusts (7:1–3)
    B. The consuming fire (7:4–6)
    C. The plumb line and opposition of Amaziah (7:7–17)
    D. The basket of fruit (8:1–14)
    E. The Lord standing beside the altar (9:1–10)
V. The restoration of Israel (9:11–15)
    A. The prophecy (9:11–12)
    B. The promise (9:13–15)

PRACTICAL ASPECTS

What impresses me as I read the Book of Amos is the fact that God is deeply involved in the lives of individuals and nations. Secular man does not have the faintest inkling of what this is all about. He is blind in his thinking, which is reflected in what he says and does.

Amos is a revelation of God's involvement in the affairs of men. None of their thoughts and actions escape His all-seeing eye. The Sovereign God knows all, sees all, hears all, and judges all. He is vitally concerned about us.

We must come to grips with this reality. By so doing, we will be the wiser and the blessed, for no person or nation can make it on their own. We need God to enlighten us, to convict us, to change us, to correct us, or else we will be eternal losers. How great that loss will be not only in time but also in eternity.

This book tells us how God feels about us, dealing with us in righteousness, justice, compassion, and mercy—to save us from eternal judgment. How good He is!

Obadiah: Wait Your Turn

The sentence of justice is always carried out in God's time not ours. Human nature demands immediacy; God says, "Wait for Me." Is it not true that the prosperity and success of the wicked make us wonder if there will ever be a divine intervention to put these things to an end?

The Book of Obadiah assures us that there will be both justice and judgment meted out to the wicked. They will have their due. Judgment of sin brings about the establishment of righteousness. Our day for deliverance from evil and its consequences is sure to come; therefore, wait your turn for blessing.

Obadiah tells us that evil is destined for destruction. Esau may do violence to Jacob, but God will deliver His people from oppression because the kingdom is His. The judgment of Esau is a harbinger of the coming judgment of the nations and the deliverance of God's people.

INFORMATIONAL MATERIAL

Obadiah is the shortest book of the Old Testament, containing only twenty-one verses and written by a man who cannot be precisely identified. He says nothing about himself in his prophecy. His is a common name among the Jews. A number of Obadiahs are mentioned in the Old Testament.

This book deals with the conflict between Edom (Esau) and Jacob (Israel). Edom is the name of a country located between the Dead Sea and the Gulf of Aqabah. It is a strip of land one hundred miles long and forty miles wide with rugged, mountainous terrain. Its inhabitants are called Edomites, descendants of Esau.

These people are in a continuing conflict with Israel, actually beginning in past generations. Before Esau and Jacob are born, the Lord reveals to Rebekah that "two nations are in your womb" (Gen. 25:23 NASB). Over the centuries, the descendants of these twin brothers are locked in a ceaseless, bloody struggle.

Obadiah's prophecy reveals that because of the arrogant spirit of the Edomites and their violence against Israel, God is going to judge them (cf. vs. 10). Their judgment results in the deliverance and blessing of Israel.

ANALYTICAL OVERVIEW

I. Superscription (1:1)
  A. The writer (1:1a)
  B. The authentic word (1:1b)
II. The judgment of Edom (1:2–14)
  A. Its certainty (1:2–4)
  B. Its severity (1:5–9)
  C. Its cause (1:10–14)
III. The judgment of the nations (1:15–16)
  A. The principle of justice (1:15)
  B. The result of judgment (1:16)

IV. The triumph of Israel (1:17–21)
   A. Victors over Esau (1:17–18)
   B. Possessors of lands (1:19–21)

PRACTICAL ASPECTS

This ancient book, with its dynamic message of "thus saith the Lord," discloses an up-to-date principle appropriate for life in our times: The Sovereign God is a God of justice, Who punishes the wicked and provides blessing for those who are His. This principle is timeless, having been in effect since the creation of mankind. This is the God to Whom all of us are accountable. Respect Him!

As you read Obadiah, with whom do you identify: Esau or Jacob? Do you see yourself in Esau with arrogance, self-sufficiency, violence, and insensitivity? Or in Jacob, perhaps distressed, but still holding onto faith and hope in God?

You see the end of both, one of judgment or one of blessing. Which will it be? It is your decision.

Jonah: Complete Your Assignment

The Book of Jonah is the test book of the Bible. Is our faith based on naturalism or supernaturalism?

Carrying a Bible in her hand, a Quaker woman on her way to church was stopped by an infidel who questioned her about the Bible. "You certainly don't believe that Bible, do you?" "I surely do," she replied, "don't thee?" "No, I don't," he answered. "You don't believe that story in there about Jonah, do you?" She said, "I surely do; don't thee?" "No, and a lot of other people don't believe it either. How do you know it is true?" "When I get to heaven, I'm going to ask him," she answered. The infidel remarked, "Well, supposing he doesn't get to heaven?" The Quaker retorted, "Then you ask him."

The Jonah story is a literal, miraculous happening throbbing with excitement. It comes about when a man given an assignment by his Lord does not want to carry it out. But God has ways—supernatural ones—to enable him to do it. After a struggle, Jonah yields to his Lord and completes the assignment. Now read all about it!

INFORMATIONAL MATERIAL

Jonah, the author of this historical narrative, is not a fictional character; his book is not a myth or an allegory. He is a prophet of God who ministers in Israel during the days of Jeroboam II (2 Kings 14:25). The prophet Amos is one of his contemporaries.

The city of Nineveh, with its teeming thousands of people located north of Babylon, is marked out by God to hear His message through Jonah. Its warlike people needed salvation. Nineveh is hundreds of miles east of Jerusalem. The other city mentioned in this book is Tarshish, situated in southern Spain.

This book has the unqualified endorsement of Jesus Christ, Who refers to Jonah as being "in the belly of the sea monster for three days and three nights" (Matt. 12:40 NASB). This experience typifies the burial and resurrection of the Savior.

Moreover, Jesus speaks of the people residing in Nineveh who "repented at the preaching of Jonah" (Matt. 12:41 NASB). These words establish the historicity and the authenticity of Jonah.

It is interesting to note that the Book of Jonah closes with a question (4:11). The only other book in the Bible that ends in like manner is Nahum (3:19). Can there be any significance to this since both books have to do with Nineveh?

ANALYTICAL OVERVIEW

I. Superscription (1:1–2)
II. Jonah's peril: running from God (1:3–17)

    A. The storm (1:3–9)
    B. The sea (1:10–16)
    C. The fish (1:17)
III. Jonah's prayer: calling on God (2:1–10)
    A. His distress (2:1–9)
    B. His deliverance (2:10)
IV. Jonah's proclamation: speaking for God (3:1–10)
    A. The message (3:1–4)
    B. The response (3:5–10)
V. Jonah's pout: complaining to God (4:1–11)
    A. His displeasure (4:1–4)
    B. His lesson (4:5–11)

PRACTICAL ASPECTS

This book is an eloquent testimony to the fact that God not only cares about His own people, Israel, but He also is concerned about the spiritual well-being of the nations. He is no respecter of persons. His love reaches out to pagan people, the most undeserving. He is not willing that any perish but that all come to repentance (2 Pet. 3:9). Jonah is the evidence of divine compassion as well as the repentant city Nineveh that experiences forgiveness.

God's goodness is seen in His response to Jonah's prayer. In his deep distress, being in pain and agony, even at the point of death, Jonah prays. He testifies: "I called . . . and He answered me" (2:2a NASB). How good God is to him. When you feel as did Jonah that it's all over or that you are abandoned, "expelled from God's sight" (2:4 NASB), *pray*. God answers the cry of distress and brings about deliverance.

The Book of Jonah proves that God is a God of grace. How patient He is in His dealings with Jonah's stubbornness. He continues working in his life and brings him to the place of great blessing. Even after this, Jonah pouts. What happens to you after God blesses you? Do you pout or praise?

Micah: Hear Your Lord

A preacher from the country shakes up a nation. Micah, from Moresheth in Judah, a little-known commoner, is making waves among an evil-thinking, idol-worshiping society. His heart-searching, simple messages are God's voice to a wayward people, who are subjects of divine judgment unless they repent.

Micah, along with Isaiah, is chosen of God to deliver His word. Both have an important ministry. Micah reaches a certain segment of the public; Isaiah, the other. The country-bred prophet Micah and the Jerusalem-born Isaiah are part of the divine strategy to communicate the "thus saith the Lord" far and wide throughout the land. Through them He will have in Isaiah access to kings and the elite; in Micah, the ordinary citizens.

Micah, who is Isaiah's younger contemporary, warns of the coming judgments to both Samaria and Jerusalem. His prophetic statements also call attention to the coming Messiah (5:2) and His glorious kingdom (4:1–8). In fact, Micah is the only Old Testament prophet who tells us of the actual birthplace of the Son of God, a prophecy uttered over seven hundred years before its fulfillment. Micah is to be trusted. Hear your Lord through His Word.

INFORMATIONAL MATERIAL

God chooses a man from a small town to accomplish a great work. Moresheth, located twenty-some miles southwest of Jerusalem, is the home of Micah.

Because Micah and Isaiah are contemporaries, their books can be studied together. At times Micah sounds like Isaiah. Can it be that he hears Isaiah speak on various occasions?

With respect to Micah's style of writing, observe that he employs repetition effectively, giving emphasis to what he says. His use of figurative expressions enables us to see the truth he proclaims.

Years after Micah concludes his ministry, the elders of Jeremiah's day quote from him (Jer. 26:18; Mic. 3:12). His prophecy of the destruction of Jerusalem comes to pass. Micah is also quoted in the New Testament (Matt. 2:6; Mic. 5:2). Jesus Himself uses a statement from Micah to emphasize His point (Matt. 10:35–36; Mic. 7:6). All of this is reliable evidence of the truthfulness and trustworthiness of this Old Testament prophetic writing.

ANALYTICAL OVERVIEW

   I. Superscription (1:1)
      A. The writer (1:1a)
      B. The times (1:1b)
      C. The message (1:1c)
  II. The Lord speaks to Samaria and Jerusalem (1:2–2:13)
      A. The announcement of judgment (1:2–6)
      B. The severity of judgment (1:7–2:5)
      C. The sins demanding judgment (2:6–11)
      D. The blessing following judgment (2:12–13)

III. The Lord speaks to leaders (3:1–12)
   A. To rulers (3:1–4)
   B. To prophets (3:5–8)
   C. To heads, rulers, priests, and prophets (3:9–12)
IV. The Lord foretells future events (4:1–5:15)
   A. The Messianic kingdom (4:1–8)
   B. The Babylonian exile (4:9–5:1)
   C. The coming Messiah (5:2–5a)
   D. The Assyrian defeat (5:5b–9)
   E. The refinement of Israel (5:10–15)
V. The Lord disputes with His people (6:1–16)
   A. His case against them (6:1–5)
   B. His requirements of them (6:6–8)
   C. His punishment for them (6:9–16)
VI. The prophet's loyalty to his Lord (7:1–20)
   A. Uncovers sin (7:1–6)
   B. Expresses faith (7:7–13)
   C. Prays (7:14–15)
   D. Honors God (7:16–20)

PRACTICAL ASPECTS

What a priceless treasure is the gift of the Word of God. It is the pearl of great price. The word of the Lord is given to Micah (1:1 NIV). This word enlightens him and makes him strong for the Lord's service. It gives him light on the present conditions of his society and insight into the future. The Psalmist declares: "The entrance of Your word gives light" (Ps. 119:130 NIV).

The Word of God through Micah is God's gift to us today. It does many wonderful things for us. It gives us insight into our own lives, who we really are and what we personally need. It shows us the kind of world we live in—one that is sinful and in need of God's saving grace. It reveals His matchless goodness in that He is forgiving, hurling "our iniquities into the depths of the sea" (7:19 NIV), forgetting them forever. In addition, the Word tells us what the future holds for the Christian. What a blessing is the gift of the Word of God. Read it daily. It works wonders in our lives.

Like Micah, Billy Graham is a country boy, given the word of the Lord. Look at what the Lord does through both of them, each in his unique way. The point, however, is that it is not the environment that makes the person; the Word of God does.

Nahum: Forsake Your Sin

Step with me into the room of a dying man without God. He is breathing heavily, struggling to hold on to life. He is surrounded by a battery of doctors and nurses. Finally, the spokesman of the group says, "There is nothing more we can do. We have tried everything possible. The patient is not responding." Moments later, the death rattle is heard. The man dies.

This is the Book of Nahum. The famous city of Nineveh, capital of Assyria, is about to die. It is impenitent. God is about to remove it from the face of the earth. It will cease to exist. Nahum prophesies this catastrophic event—the death of a city. History confirms it.

Over many years God is patient with the city, sending Jonah there to preach repentance. Nineveh responds by repenting and is spared. Nevertheless, it lapses into abominable vices and is now ready for judgment. God visits this city with righteous wrath. It is about to be destroyed.

Mercy does not attend its funeral, for the time comes when God says, "That's enough." The day of grace is gone forever. Do not let this happen to you. Forsake your sin and believe on Jesus Christ and you will be saved.

INFORMATIONAL MATERIAL

The word "oracle" is used by the prophets to denote a divine utterance, a message coming from God. Sometimes the word "burden" is used to reveal the same thing (1:1 NKJV). God is laying a "heavy" on the people. They should take the truth seriously, giving it their undivided attention.

The writer of this book, Nahum, is unknown, and the place of his birth has been the object of scholars' investigations. No positive identification has yet been made of the hometown Elkosh.

Nahum is a gifted word artist. On a scroll, he puts various combinations of words together, enabling one to see the truth, making these word pictures vivid, impressive, and unforgettable. We are made to marvel at them.

In Nahum we are aware of the gathering storm of divine judgment. We can almost hear the rumble of the thunder in the distance and see the lightning flash across angry clouds. Nahum gives us a realistic picture of a coming judgment day. Prepare for it.

ANALYTICAL OVERVIEW

I. Superscription (1:1)
II. The revelation of God (1:2–2:2)
   A. His person (1:2–3)
   B. His power (1:4–6)
   C. His predetermination (1:7–2:2)
III. The destruction of Nineveh (2:3–3:19)
   A. The city invaded (2:3–7)
   B. The treasures sacked (2:8–13)
   C. The battle described (3:1–4)

D. The punishment foretold (3:5–7)
E. The devastation depicted (3:8–19)

PRACTICAL ASPECTS

Nahum gives us a revelation of the character of God—a God of holiness with righteous wrath, a God of love with redeeming grace for the repentant. Whereas the emphasis of Nahum is on the justification of God's intense hatred of and anger against sin—resulting ultimately in deliverance of His people Israel from the enemy—there is also a manifestation of His mercy and goodness.

The following expressions give support to this concept: "The Lord is slow to anger" (1:3); "The Lord is good" (1:7); and "The Lord will restore the splendor of Jacob" (2:2 NASB).

The God of the twentieth century has not changed over the course of time. He is eternally the same, the God of love and the God of wrath. This is the God all of us must deal with and be subject to. The twentieth century mind-set may think of God only in terms of love, but this is a half-truth. We must believe all the Bible says of Him.

What is your belief in God? Is it based on full truth or half-truth?

Habakkuk: Ask Your Questions

Have you ever asked God some questions about disturbing matters that deeply hurt you? I am sure you have. I have, too. The man of God, Habakkuk, also has questions to ask God. Is it wrong to ask questions of God? Is it unspiritual? Is it a revelation of a weakness of character? I think not.

Actually, asking questions depends upon our attitude. If our attitude is one of skepticism, defiance, and unbelief, it is an affront to God. If it is one of honesty that comes from our heart in a spirit of humility, the Lord will respond to us in His way and in His time.

In what kind of spirit do you ask God questions? This is all-important to receiving His answer. I believe the Lord so graciously responds to Habakkuk's questions because he is honest, open, truthful, and obedient. He receives God's answers and rejoices in Him for them (3:18).

INFORMATIONAL MATERIAL

Little is known about the prophet Habakkuk. From the content of his prophecy regarding the Babylonian invasion, in all probability he is a contemporary of Jeremiah.

Certainly, he is a gifted writer and a herald of hope. He looks ahead and declares: "The earth will be filled with the knowledge of the glory of the Lord, as the waters cover the sea" (2:14 NASB). And even in the times of judgment, he recognizes that God is ruling: "But the Lord is in His holy temple. Let all the earth be silent before Him" (2:20 NASB).

Habakkuk begins with a sigh but ends with a song. It opens with a dilemma but closes with certainty. Habakkuk deals honestly both with faith's interrogations and faith's affirmations.

The Lord lays down a principle in this book that is used three times in the New Testament: "The righteous will live by his faith" (2:4 NASB). Paul picks up this expression in Romans 1:17 as he writes of the gospel of Christ. To the Galatians, he declares that justification is possible only through faith (3:11). The writer to the Hebrews quotes this truth also (10:38).

ANALYTICAL OVERVIEW

I. Superscription (1:1)
    A. The oracle (1:1a)
    B. The writer (1:1b)
II. Habakkuk's first prayer (1:1–4)
    A. His questions (1:2–3)
    B. His observations (1:4)
III. The Lord's response (1:5–11)
    A. The Chaldeans are selected (1:5–6)
    B. The Chaldeans are described (1:7–11)
IV. Habakkuk's second prayer (1:12–2:1)
    A. His questions (1:12–14)
    B. His concerns (1:15–17)
    C. His faith (2:1)

V. The Lord's response (2:2–20)
    A. Instructions for Habakkuk (2:2–3)
    B. Judgment for the Chaldeans (2:4–20)
VI. Habakkuk's third prayer (3:1–2b)
    A. His respect (3:1–2a)
    B. His request (3:2b)
VII. The Lord's response (3:3–15)
    A. A revelation of His glory (3:3–4)
    B. A revelation of His power (3:5–15)
VIII. Habakkuk's faith (3:16–19)
    A. He will wait for God (3:16–17)
    B. He will rejoice in God (3:18–19)

PRACTICAL ASPECTS

The very fact that God gives us the Book of Habakkuk is evidence that He understands us with our perplexities and problems. To turn Godward with our questions is always the right thing to do. He Who is infinite in knowledge knows us perfectly and knows what we deeply feel and what we really need. He sees what we do not see at the moment. He knows what should be done in His time. He has unlimited power to do it. Habakkuk finds this to be true; so will we.

What a high honor and great privilege it is to come to our Lord with honest, perhaps disturbing or distressing, questions. He has answers for us. To receive them, we must follow the example of Habakkuk and not be impatient. Does he not say, "I will wait patiently" (3:16 NIV)?

To wait patiently means to be sensitive to His providence, to walk in His light, and to love Him supremely. In so doing, we discover that what is incomprehensible becomes plain. Our gracious Lord turns our perplexities into praises.

Zephaniah: Change Your Course

Like a blind man about to step over a precipice are Judah and Jerusalem, hand in hand, heading for the brink of disaster and destruction. In that fateful moment, God raises up Zephaniah to call out, "Stop! Change your course. You are headed for judgment."

The nation needs to hear the message loud and clear; and God gives it to them through Zephaniah, who calls attention to the sovereignty of God, the sins of the people, the reality of judgment, the call to repentance, and the promise of a new day. The Lord does everything possible to arouse His people to turn to Him. If they seek Him, He will be merciful. If not, they must bear sin's consequences.

It is just this simple. Man has a choice to make. His choice leads to a destiny. What happens to him, then, is not the fault of his Maker but of his own personal decision.

Zephaniah enables us to see life in this light.

INFORMATIONAL MATERIAL

Apparently, Zephaniah has royal blood in his veins if he is the great-great-grandson of Hezekiah the king. Moreover, this makes him a distant relative of King Josiah. His residence is probably Jerusalem.

Second Kings 22:1–23:30 and 2 Chronicles 34:1–35:27 give us a picture of the times in which Zephaniah prophesies. The reign of King Josiah lasts thirty-one years. It is during this time that Jeremiah also prophesies.

In Zephaniah the word "day" is used many times as is the expression "I will." The "day" refers to "the day of the Lord," which relates to the time of God's wrath and judgment. One instance of "day" speaks of the Lord's mercy (3:16).

The "I will" indicates God's sovereignty. He is in charge of His people and the nations, exercising supreme control over them, allowing them to continue only as long as He determines. Every sinful society is destroyed in God's time. History confirms this.

ANALYTICAL OVERVIEW

I. Superscription (1:1)
    A. The writer (1:1a)
    B. The genealogy (1:1b)
    C. The time frame (1:1c)
II. The determination of the Lord (1:2–6)
    A. To judge Judah and Jerusalem (1:2–4a)
    B. To deal with sinners (1:4b–6)
III. The Day of the Lord (1:7–2:3)
    A. The time of judgment (1:7–13)
    B. The description of judgment (1:14–18)
    C. The call to repentance (2:1–3)
IV. The destruction of the nations (2:4–15)
    A. Philistia (2:4–7)
    B. Moab and Ammon (2:8–11)
    C. Ethiopia (2:12)
    D. Assyria (2:13–15)

PRACTICAL ASPECTS

Our society desperately needs to read the prophets in order to have a high view of God. Modern man's thoughts of Him are distorted and unrealistic. Our Lord truly is the God of love, but He is infinitely more. He is holy, righteous, just, exalted. No human vocabulary can describe Him.

The Bible tells us Who He is, what He is like, and what He does. He is our Creator, and we are accountable to Him. Zephaniah tells us about His wrath and His mercy. Wrath is poured out on the transgressor. Mercy abounds to the one who repents.

Therefore what happens to us—wrath or mercy—is based on our decision. God does not make us machines, robots programmed to love Him and to carry out His desires. He makes us free moral agents with a will that can respond to Him or reject Him. He forces no one to love Him. That is our decision. We have been given freedom—freedom that carries responsibility that will be called into account on Judgment Day.

I have made my decision to receive Christ and His matchless mercy. I hope you will do the same.

Haggai: Finish Your Work

This small book packs a powerful punch. It is more than a gentle nudge. It may be likened to a dynamite blast, freeing the Lord's people from icy indifference. Striking to the very heart of a careless society, it is especially effective. Dynamic, indeed, is the Lord's word. When He speaks, mountains melt, nations shake, and people move.

The Lord comes on the scene, as Haggai puts it, during the second year of the reign of Darius. Four different times God speaks that year, twice in one day (2:10, 20). He gives His Word through the prophet to the leaders of the nation, Zerubbabel and Joshua, and to all the people.

Things happen. Attitudes change. People work. The temple is finished (Ezra 6:14–15). What joy and blessedness follows. In these historic circumstances, the changes go from bad to good, from smoldering coals to flaming fire. The crowd catches the Spirit of God; rather, the Spirit of God captures them, freeing them to do His will, to complete the work on the temple. How good and wonderful it is.

Oh, the power of four short messages from God.

INFORMATIONAL MATERIAL

The Book of Ezra serves as an excellent and accurate source of information for the background of Haggai (cf. Ezra 1–6).

Although Haggai is mentioned by name in Ezra 5:1 and 6:14, and in his own book eight times, little is known about his personal life.

Perhaps God keeps His servant in obscurity so that we will not think more of him than of the word of the Lord he declares. The Book of Haggai has an authoritative tone since it comes from the Lord. Many expressions such as "the word of the Lord came," "declares the Lord," and "declares the Lord Almighty" (NIV) are used twenty-five times throughout the book. Haggai is merely the channel through whom God speaks.

Not only is God speaking, but He is also working through leaders—Zerubbabel, the governor; Joshua, the priest; and many people. As a result the temple is rebuilt.

ANALYTICAL OVERVIEW

I. Superscription (1:1)
    A. The time factor (1:1a)
    B. The writer (1:1b)
    C. The addressees (1:1c)
II. The first message (1:2–15)
    A. The awakening call (1:2–6)
    B. The chastening drought (1:7–11)
    C. The heartening response (1:12–15)
III. The second message (2:1–9)
    A. The exhortation (2:1–5)

B. The promise (2:6–9)
IV. The third message (2:10–19)
    A. The questions and answers (2:10–14)
    B. The promise of better times (2:15–19)
V. The fourth message (2:20–23)
    A. The shaking of the nations (2:20–22)
    B. The promise to Zerubbabel (2:23)

PRACTICAL ASPECTS

How the people need to hear the message of Haggai. Having returned to Judah and Jerusalem from the Babylonian captivity, they start working on rebuilding the Lord's house, but because of severe opposition, they stop.

Sixteen years pass and nothing is done. In the meantime, the people build their own houses and till the soil. Becoming preoccupied with their self-centered interests, they neglect the house of the Lord. In this state "the bombshell drops"— the word of God comes to them through Haggai. How powerful it is. It motivates them to put God first.

Nothing is as effective as the Word of God to get people into the right frame of mind and to move them from a state of lethargy to one of holy passion.

When we find ourselves losing interest in the things of God, becoming stale spiritually, feeling dull and down, we must get in touch with the Word of God. It does wonders for us, bringing refreshment into our life and causing our desert to blossom like a rose. We will be strengthened and encouraged to finish the work the Lord gives us to do.

Zechariah: Mine Your Gold

Zechariah is a gold mine of prophetic truth concerning the first and second coming of Jesus Christ. In order to get the gold from this prophecy, we must dig deep by spending time in a careful study of it. Upon reaching and grasping these golden truths, we become spiritually rich indeed.

The message of Zechariah, though having future implications, is relevant to the people of his times because it activates them to get on with the work of the Lord. For many years nothing is being done, but now through Zechariah a fresh vision provides inspiration to the people. The work on the temple is completed.

Also, there are significant future activities planned by God as envisioned by the prophet—events that will take place in the end times. Therefore, this prophecy takes on a fuller and deeper meaning for all God's people because it presents a worldview: There will be a literal kingdom of God on earth with headquarters in Jerusalem under the Lordship of Jesus Christ (14:9).

Informational Material

Zechariah and Haggai are contemporaries, ministering in the same historical situation. Both prophets render outstanding service in an ongoing work of the Lord.

Like the Book of Haggai, Zechariah's prophecies have an authoritative tone. The expressions, "the word of the Lord came," "thus says the Lord of hosts," and "declares the Lord," are found fifty-seven times.

Another significant expression, "in that day," is found seventeen times in chapters twelve through fourteen. It refers to eschatological events taking place in the end times.

Like Daniel and Ezekiel, Zechariah is an apocalyptic writing, characterized by visions, angels, symbols, and prophecies. Such writings are used to bring encouragement to God's people.

The New Testament contains quotations from Zechariah: Christ's triumphal entry into the city of Jerusalem (9:9; Matt. 21:5; John 12:15); and His message to His disciples on the night of His betrayal (13:7; Matt. 26:31; Mark 14:27).

Our Lord speaks of Zechariah by name, telling of his death by martyrdom (Matt. 23:35). Thus, does Jesus Christ Himself validate the historicity of Zechariah.

Analytical Overview

I. Introduction (1:1–6)
   A. The writer (1:1)
   B. The exhortation (1:2–6)
II. The visions and prophecies of Zechariah (1:7–6:15)
   A. The rider on the red horse (1:7–17)

B. The four horns and the four craftsmen (1:18–21)
C. The man with the measuring line (2:1–13)
D. The high priest Joshua (3:1–10)
E. The golden lampstand and the two olive trees (4:1–14)
F. The flying scroll (5:1–4)
G. The ephod and the woman (5:5–11)
H. The four chariots (6:1–8)
I. A symbolical action pointing to the Branch (6:9–15)

III. The inquiry from Bethel (7:1–8:23)
A. The question (7:1–3)
B. The response (7:4–14)
C. The promises (8:1–23)

IV. The severity and kindness of God (9:1–11:17)
A. The judgment of nations (9:1–8)
B. The prophecy of the King (9:9–10)
C. The deliverance of Israel (9:11–10:12)
D. The allegory of the shepherds (11:1–17)

V. The word concerning Israel (12:1–14:21)
A. The battle over Jerusalem (12:1–14)
B. The cleansing of Israel (13:1–9)
C. The coming of the King (14:1–8)
D. The establishment of the kingdom (14:9–21)

PRACTICAL ASPECTS

The reading of the Old Testament is very difficult for some, but that does not suggest it should be avoided. We need to remember that Zechariah is part of the divine revelation also.

It is good for us to read the truths we do not readily understand. This makes us think and pray for enlightenment. Our Lord does not put everything in apple-pie order that we may hurry our way through the Word; nor is the Bible like a fast-food drive-in—a McDonald's where we may get our spiritual food on the run.

Moreover, He does not spoon-feed us. We are not to be little children in the faith all our lives. We are not to remain kindergartners. We are to grow, mature, and develop spiritually and intellectually. This is why it is necessary to read what is challenging, not only what is easy. After all, both easily understood truths and difficult ones are in the Bible.

Read them all. Reading Zechariah stretches us spiritually. We will find gold—if we dig deep enough.

Malachi: Show Your Colors

On an autumn afternoon in a football stadium, two great teams, Army and Notre Dame, were in the middle of a bruising battle. During the first half, Knute Rockne, coach of the Irish, noticed that one of his good linemen was not playing up to his potential. This gave him deep concern.

During half-time, Rockne was able to borrow one of Army's jerseys. Coming into the locker room just before the team was ready to return to the field, he took the Army jersey and flung it into the face of the player who was not giving his best and said, "Here, put this on. You're playing better for Army than you are for us."

The young man got the message and for the rest of the game gave it all he had. What a difference his playing made for the coach, the team, and himself.

Like this young athlete, the nation of Israel is letting down spiritually and needs to come to grips with its waywardness—its irreverence, its indifference, and its indulgence in sin. God raises up Malachi to declare His message, which is terse and heartsearching, probing deep into the inner life and outward conduct.

Israel must take the Lord seriously—turn from sin, return to Him, and show the true colors of love and loyalty to

God. Otherwise, they play into the hand of the enemy, hurt the Lord's cause, and suffer eternal loss.

INFORMATIONAL MATERIAL

While Malachi gives the message to Israel, he uses a dialogical methodology. Hailey calls it

> a new style of address known as the didactic-dialectic method of speaking. In this type of teaching, an assertion or charge is made, a fancied objection is raised by the hearers, and a refutation to the objection is presented by the speaker.[37]

The Book of Malachi contains fifty-five verses in which various expressions such as "says the Lord" and similar ones are mentioned twenty-five times. God speaks through His servant. Here again, divine authority is in evidence.

This message is greatly needed for Malachi's day—and ours. Although the priests and people have lost their fear of God and have drifted far from Him, He still loves them. Out of His love come words of condemnation for evil practices, the call to repentance, warnings of judgment, and promises of blessing.

Malachi, a prophet like so many others, is an unknown. His is the last word of the prophets of the Old Testament. For four hundred years there will be no prophetic vision or voice. God has spoken precisely and loudly over the years through many of His messengers. The next time He speaks is in His Son, Whose way is prepared by His forerunner, John the Baptist.

ANALYTICAL OVERVIEW

I. Introduction (1:1–5)
   A. God's word through Malachi (1:1)
   B. God's love for Jacob (1:2)
   C. God's judgment of Esau (1:3–5)
II. The word of the Lord to the priests (1:6–2:9)
   A. The sins of the priests (1:6–14)
   B. The warning of judgment (2:1–9)
III. The word of the Lord to the people (2:10–4:3)
   A. The sins of the people (2:10–17)
   B. The prophecy of the Lord's coming (3:1–6)
   C. The promise of blessing (3:7–12)
   D. The importance of a holy fear (3:13–4:3)
IV. Conclusion (4:4–6)
   A. The exhortation to obedience (4:4)
   B. The promise to send Elijah (4:5–6)

PRACTICAL ASPECTS

Spiritual slippage is one of the dominant characteristics of every generation. Is it not easier to take the way of least resistance? This is true in the days of Malachi and also in ours. It takes divine strength to go against the tide—the majority, whose philosophy is "Everyone else is doing it; why shouldn't I?"

Malachi is well aware of the spiritual lapses of God's people, both in leaders and in laity, who are not what they should be. Failing to take the Lord and His Word seriously, they become irreverent, careless, arrogant, and self-sufficient. The results are disastrous.

This is why we must keep up our guard, lest we become like everyone else. Eternal vigilance is the price of liberty in the gospel. Therefore, watch your actions—what you do. Watch your attitudes—what you think. Watch your words—what you say. This is not a religion of works but of the faith that produces good works. Faith in Jesus Christ, plus nothing, saves us; but works give evidence of our salvation. This is in keeping with New Testament teaching, for James says, "Faith without works is dead" (James 2:26).

How does your spiritual life square with Malachi and James?

THE NEW TESTAMENT BOOKS

"Therefore everyone who hears these words of mine and puts them into practice is like a wise man who built his house on a rock." (Matt. 7:24, NIV)

Matthew: Magnify Your Messiah

A tax-collector sitting in his office hears the invitation of the Savior. Responding immediately, Matthew leaves everything to follow the Messiah. He becomes the penman of the gospel bearing his name.

The gospel according to Matthew is the good news of Jesus the Christ, the beloved Son of God, Who came to earth for the purpose of redeeming lost mankind by giving His life "as a ransom . . ." (20:28). Jesus is the Savior, the Anointed One, the Messiah, Who is Prophet, Priest, and King. That He is all of this and infinitely more is prefigured and predicted in the Old Testament.

Matthew's emphasis is on the works and words of the Messiah, Jesus Christ. Scroggie observes that one-fourth of the gospel is taken up with Christ's words.[38]

The Messiah is God Himself, manifested in human flesh; therefore, let us magnify, extol, hold in greater esteem, and respect Him Who suffered, bled, died, and rose again to make possible a salvation that sets us free from sin and gives us a new song.

Informational Material

Matthew possesses a methodical mind, having had to work with figures and to make out reports. This ability, now under God's supervision, is reflected in his writing. Scholars observe that he writes in threes (e.g., the threefold division of chronology [1:17]; three temptations [4:1–11]; three illustrations of righteousness, three prohibitions, and three commands [7:1–9:34]).

There are five discourses of Jesus Christ presented in this gospel: the Sermon on the Mount (5:1–7:29); the commission to the twelve apostles (10:1–42); the parables (13:1–53); the message on humility and forgiveness (18:1–35); and eschatological truths (24:1–25:46). Each discourse is preceded by a narrative section. This pattern indicates the stately structure of the Gospel.

Matthew uses the word "fulfill" many times to prove that the Messiah of Whom he writes is the subject of many prophecies found in the Old Testament. Matthew serves as a bridge or connecting link between the Old and the New Testaments. "The major events in the life of Jesus took place in fulfillment of prophecy."[39] Another has said that "No Gospel links together so closely the Old and New Testaments; and no document in the New Testament sets forth the person of Jesus and His life and teaching, so clearly as the fulfillment of 'the law and the prophets.'"[40]

"That it might be fulfilled which was spoken by the prophet, saying, . . ." is mentioned at least eleven times.

In this gospel the authority of the Messiah is clearly seen. Many times the expressions, "I tell you" and "I tell you the truth" are used. Little wonder, then, that after hearing Jesus, "the crowds were amazed at his teaching, because he taught as one who had authority, and not as their teachers of the law" (7:28–29 NIV).

Although the Gospel is intended for Jewish Christians in order that they might be grounded in the faith and have a proper view of Jesus Christ, it is also for the Gentiles. They are not bypassed. In the tables of genealogy (chapter one), Matthew shows that Gentile blood is in the ancestral line of Christ. Rahab and Ruth are mentioned specifically (1:5). Jesus goes outside Galilee to minister in Tyre and Sidon (15:21–28). Specifically, in the Great Commission, all peoples of the world are included in the plan of God; salvation is for all mankind, not just the Jews (28:18–20).

Harrison noted that Matthew's Gospel "has the same general purpose as the others, to set forth such a knowledge of Jesus Christ and His work as to make possible an intelligent decision for Him and the gospel. But in an exceptional way, this Gospel seems intended to serve as a teaching manual for the church."[41]

ANALYTICAL OVERVIEW

I. The majesty of the Messiah (1:1–4:25)
   A. His ancestry (1:1–17)
   B. His nativity (1:18–26)
   C. His infancy (2:1–22)
   D. His identity (3:1–17)
   E. His victory (4:1–11)
   F. His ministry (4:12–25)
II. The message of Messiah (5:1–7:29)
   A. The subjects of the kingdom (5:1–16)
   B. The standards of the kingdom (5:17–7:12)
   C. The seekers of the kingdom (7:13–23)

D. The strength of the kingdom (7:24–29)
III. The ministry of Messiah (8:1–25:46)
    A. His ministry in Galilee (8:1–18:35)
        NOTE: *Jesus withdrew from Galilee to Syrophoen-icia (15:21–28) and to Caesarea Philippi (16:13–17:23)*
    B. His ministry in Perea (19:1–20:16)
    C. His ministry in Jerusalem (20:17–25:46)
IV. The mediation of Messiah (26:1–28:20)
    A. Submission (26:1–27:31)
    B. Crucifixion (27:32–65)
    C. Resurrection (28:1–20)

PRACTICAL ASPECTS

Jesus attracts needy people (8:1). The leper comes to Him for help (8:2); so does a centurion (8:5), as well as many others (8:16). Jesus helps those who are in need. Those needs may be great, but His supply is limitless. "In the heart of a man a cry, in the heart of God supply."

God uses redeemed people with developed characters to accomplish His plans and purposes. Righteous Joseph and blameless Mary are chosen to be the earthly parents of the beloved Son of God. They are prepared for their high calling, being self-controlled, submissive, and obedient to their Lord.

The will of God is accomplished through men and women of high moral and spiritual character, individuals who will not cut corners, carry out under-the-table deals, and not compromise biblical principles.

Go with God just one step at a time. Joseph did. Mary did. Consequently, they are always at the right place at the right time. Read Psalm 37:23. There is no better way of life than living in the will of God.

Jesus Christ never acts or speaks contrary to the Scriptures. He gives insight into them, enabling us to have a better understanding of them. He highly regards the Word of God. What an example for New Testament believers— *never* to belittle the Old Testament revelation but to respect it, read it, and practice it in New Testament light.

People living in New Testament times are going to receive greater judgment than those under the Old Testament covenant. The reason for this difference is the degree of light that we have received. Light determines the intensity of judgment. All sin will be judged; nothing will be overlooked by a holy God (Luke 12:47–48). This truth Jesus Himself teaches in Matthew 11:20–24. Great light makes a great sinner, resulting in great judgment.

Matthew clearly identifies Jesus Christ, Messiah. There is no one like Him. Truly He is Godman: therefore, magnify the Messiah.

Mark: Mind Your Master

C an you imagine a master becoming a servant? Certainly the rulers of this world do not think in these terms. However, Jesus Christ the King of Glory is Totally Other. In keeping with Old Testament prophecy He becomes the Servant of God.

Mark portrays Jesus Christ as Master of mankind and as Servant of God in his Gospel. The content of the book indicates that Jesus Christ is in absolute control of every situation with which He is confronted, whether it be instructing His disciples, healing those with dreaded diseases, or silencing His critics. Furthermore His sovereign power is seen in the realm of nature as He rebukes wild winds and waves. He confronts demonic spirits fearlessly, rebuking them forthrightly and giving them orders to leave their victims immediately.

As Servant, Jesus Christ gives Himself untiringly and selflessly to reach fallen, hopeless souls with the good news of the kingdom, to instruct His disciples, and to heal the sick. He walks the dusty roads, prays in lonely places, sails stormy seas, and preaches in cities and villages in order to serve. Mark calls this Master of men, "the Son of Man." At the same time, He is the Son of God. What a perfect Godman—Master and Servant!

Informational Material

The Gospel of Mark is the shortest of the four Gospels, but certainly no less important or inferior in its content. He does not give the details of other gospel writers. He seems to be in a hurry to tell the story of Jesus Christ. This is such good news, it must be told. He uses the word meaning "immediately," "forthwith," or "straightaway" some forty-one times. This is a book of action. Jesus is going places and doing things.

Scholarly research indicates that Mark's Gospel contains many truths found in Peter's preaching. According to Irenaeus, one of the early church fathers, "Mark, the disciple and interpreter of Peter, also transmitted to us in writing what had been preached by Peter."[42]

Erdman suggests that

> Mark is the Gospel for youth; it is so brief, so vivid, so stirring, so strong; and these same qualities adapt the story to the active, restless, vigorous spirit of the whole modern world. . . .
>
> This Gospel is one of miracles rather than parables; of the former nineteen are recorded, two of which are peculiar to Mark, while of the latter we find only four.[43]

Mark reports on the last week of Jesus in Jerusalem. This material (11:1–16:8) comprises over one-third of the content of the book.

Kerr observes that

> Mark unfolds the truth more in acts than in words. He "frames a series of word pictures . . ." With a stroke of the pen he gives us a word picture of some action or

look of the Savior, and thus gives us a new insight into the gracious manner of Christ."[44]

"Mark is a Gospel of personal reactions," says Tenney. "All through its pages are recorded the responses of Jesus' audience. They were 'amazed' (1:27), 'critical' (2:7), 'afraid' (4:41), 'puzzled' (6:14), 'astonished' (7:37), 'bitterly hostile' (14:1). There are at least twenty-three such references."[45]

The suffering, death, and resurrection of Jesus Christ is mentioned many times by the Savior Himself (8:31; 9:9, 31; 10:32–34; 14:22–28). Therefore the cross is neither an accident nor a surprise to Christ. He fully expects it; He comes to die.

Mark's Gospel is an evangelistic appeal to mankind to trust Jesus Christ as Savior and Lord.

ANALYTICAL OVERVIEW

I. The magnificence of the Master (1:1–13)
   A. Based on Old Testament prophecy (1:1–3)
   B. Announced by John the Baptizer (1:4–8)
   C. Confirmed by God the Father (1:9–11)
   D. Questioned by Satan the tempter (1:12–13)
II. The ministry of the Master (1:14–14:42)
   A. His ministry prior to Jerusalem (1:14–10:52)
   B. His ministry in Jerusalem (11:1–14:42)
III. The mistreatment of the Master (14:43–15:47)
   A. His arrest (14:43–52)
   B. His trials (14:53–15:20)
   C. His crucifixion (15:21–41)
   D. His death and burial (15:42–47)

IV. The mightiness of the Master (16:1–20)
   A. Power over death—the empty tomb (16:1–6)
   B. Power of life—the risen Lord (16:7–20)

Practical Aspects

In reading Mark's Gospel, we get the impression that Jesus Christ is in control. He is Master with limitless authority. Those who listen to His messages acknowledge that "He taught them as one who had authority" (1:22). In speaking to the healed paralytic, Jesus says, "I tell you, get up, take your mat and go home" (2:11). To evil spirits, Jesus "gives strict orders not to tell who He was" (3:12). The frightened disciples know that "even the wind and the waves obey Him" (4:41). Even His critics have to recognize His authority; they ask, "And who gave you authority to do this?" (11:28). As Master, Jesus never allows Himself to be put on the defensive. He does not bend to the pressure of a critic. The Master is in charge.

The example of Christ in dealing with persons who experience His healing touch should be carefully followed today. He does not permit the healed person to remain in the crowd; He sends him away immediately. This suggests that Jesus never makes an exhibition of a healed person. He does not say, "Look here. See this healed person. Give God a hand." How wise is Jesus. He does not expect faith to be based on what we see, but on His Word, on Himself. Had Jesus made a spectacle of the healed person, it would have drawn attention away from the Healer.

We must go by the Word of God—His commandments—and not the traditions of men (7:1–13). Tradition, too often, is based on man-made rules. The commandments are from God.

Jesus seems to have had a particular fondness for the Sea of Galilee. This sea is special and significant to Him. He walks on it. He sails across it often. He stills its storms. He calls His disciples from its shores. He makes possible miraculous catches of fish; the life in the sea is tamed by Him. He appears to His disciples in His resurrected glory by the Sea of Galilee.

How vitally important it is to believe God. Jesus teaches, "Have faith in God" (11:22); "All things are possible with God" (10:27). Those who believe see the salvation of the Lord; those who do not believe miss the glory of the Lord. This is what happens during the last week of the Master's ministry in Jerusalem. During this time there is intense hostility against Jesus; consequently, no miracle is recorded by Mark for individuals. Only one miracle is performed by Christ's sovereignty: the cursing of the fig tree (11:12–14, 20). No miracles are performed for those with a spirit of hostility against the Master.

Jesus loves the children (9:36; 10:14–16). Boys and girls are precious to Him. Are they precious to you?

Ministry for the Master takes place wherever the minister/servant is. How true this is in the life of Christ. He does not confine His work within the walls of the synagogue. In fact, more is done outside the synagogue than inside. He calls His disciples by the seaside (1:16). He heals Peter's mother-in-law in a house (1:31). He prays on the mountain (1:35). He seeks to save sinners at a dinner in Levi's home (2:15–17). He heals a woman in the street (5:34). He ministers in the marketplace (6:56). We can have a ministry anywhere—in the church, in the home, in the office, at the college, on the football field, at sea, on ocean, on the plane—wherever we are as we mind our Master!

Luke: Revere Your Redeemer

L uke, the beloved physician, is one of the four biographers of the life of Christ. His insightful mind and keen love of truth is reflected in his inspired writing. In following the general pattern of Matthew and Mark, Luke gives us an orderly account of the life of our Lord Jesus Christ as Redeemer, from His prenatal days to His majestic ascension into heaven. Luke's primary purpose in writing is to assure the followers of Christ that their faith is based on absolutes, centering in the person of Jesus Christ.

Luke identifies divine truth with historical persons and places to validate that what he is saying is not a fable, a theory, a philosophy, or a myth. This actually happened in history. Our salvation is in the historical Person Jesus Christ, Who steps out of eternity into time at birth and returns to the eternal heavenly realm at His ascension. Our Redeemer is real; revere Him.

INFORMATIONAL MATERIAL

The Gospel of Luke is the most beautiful book ever written. The author is a gifted painter of word pictures and has been described as the most literary author of the New Testament.[46] His Gospel is the most complete account of the life of Jesus Christ; it gives details that other Gospel writers are not led to include in their accounts. Luke's Gospel contains more parables than either Matthew, Mark, or John. There are traces of his medical knowledge observed in his Gospel as he tells of the miracles of healing (4:38; 5:12; 8:43; 13:11).

Luke is a first-rate historian. Kerr calls him the "Father of Christian Church history."[47] His facts are not simply a record of dull happenings; rather, they are live interpretations.

Luke is an outstanding evangelist. He writes to win the lost for the heavenly kingdom. He declares forthrightly, "For the Son of Man came to seek and to save what was lost" (19:10). In three parables he tells of the joyous celebration that takes place when sinners repent (chapter 15).

In reading the Gospel of Luke one will observe that a spirit of joy dominates many accounts; (e.g., joy at the birth of John [1:64]; joy of Elizabeth [1:58]; joy of Mary [1:46–47]; joy of the shepherds (2:20); joy of Simeon and Anna [2:28, 38]. The Gospel begins and ends with rejoicing [1:47; 24:52–53]). Luke records joyful sounds.

The Holy Spirit is given a prominent place in the unfolding narrative of the Good News. There are many references to Him (1:15, 35, 41, 67; 2:25–27; 3:16, 22; 4:1, 18; 11:13; 12:10, 12).

Luke emphasizes the teaching and praying ministry of the Redeemer. Jesus teaches in the synagogues of Galilee (4:15); while seated in a boat (5:1–3); in a house (5:17–19); while journeying to Jerusalem (13:10); and in the Temple (19:47; 20:1; 21:37). Jesus is a praying teacher (5:16; 6:12; 9:18).

Womanhood is honored by Luke as he depicts the devotion of women to their Lord. They are given a prominent place in his Gospel (e.g., Elizabeth, the mother of John [1:13]; Mary, the mother of Jesus [1:27–28]; Anna, the prophetess [2:36]; Mary and Martha [10:38–42]; Mary Magdalene [8:2]; Joanna, wife of Chuza, Herod's steward [8:3]; Susanna [8:3]). Women follow Jesus to the cross and witness His crucifixion (23:27). Women announce the resurrection to the disciples (24:10).

ANALYTICAL OVERVIEW

I. Introduction (1:1–4)
II. The advent of the Redeemer (1:5–4:13)
   A. Preceded by John the Baptizer (1:5–25)
   B. Determined by God the Father (1:26–56)
   C. Fulfilled in historical times (2:1–4:13)
III. The accomplishments of the Redeemer (4:14–23:56)
   A. His ministry in Galilee (4:14–9:50)
   B. His ministry enroute to Jerusalem (9:51–19:27)
   C. His ministry in Jerusalem (19:28–23:56)
      NOTE: *This section tells of the events of the last week of Christ's ministry, beginning in triumph and ending in tragedy, followed by the resurrection victory.*
IV. The acclamation of the Redeemer (24:1–53)
   A. The announcement of His resurrection (24:1–12)
   B. The assurance of His resurrection (24:13–49)
   C. The ascension after His resurrection (24:50–53)

PRACTICAL ASPECTS

In Luke's Gospel the Lord blesses and uses both the young and old (1:26–38; 2:25–38). To young people,

Joseph and Mary—righteous, obedient, and believing—God commits the care of His beloved Son during His formative years from infancy to adolescence. To the aged Simeon and Anna—full of the Holy Spirit and obedient to Him—the Lord reveals Himself, giving them insight into His plans and purposes. The church needs quality youth to carry heavy loads of responsibility. It equally needs the elderly to counsel and give stability. God blends the young and the old together in carrying out His will.

The Word of God is given to us in order that we might have our faith strengthened, being assured that what we have come to believe is true and right (1:1–4). The good news concerning Jesus Christ is historically true and precisely correct. The Psalmist puts it like this: "Your word, O Lord, is eternal; it stands firm in the heavens" (Ps. 119:89 NIV).

Waiting for God's time is exceedingly difficult because it requires great patience. There is a four hundred year waiting period between the Old and New Testaments. After Jesus is born, people have to wait thirty years before receiving His public ministry (3:23). The things God does for us do not happen overnight, or even in one year's time. Therefore, we must be patient in our believing, as the biblical writer explains that it is through faith and patience we inherit what has been promised (Heb. 6:12). "And so after waiting patiently, Abraham received what was promised" (Heb. 6:15 NIV). The time element is with God; the faith and patience element with us.

Guard against unbelief and hostility toward God. During the last week of Christ's earthly ministry, few miracles are performed. In fact, Luke records only one healing, that of the restoration of the high priest's servant's ear (22:51). The scribes, Pharisees, and Sadducees experience nothing of Christ's dynamic workings because of their unbelief, hostility, and murderous intent. The lesson is plain: Those who challenge Christ will never know the power of Christ.

Revere your Redeemer. Honor Him. Love Him. Feel kindly disposed toward Him. Believe Him. Can we really do anything less? Luke's good news tells us Who Jesus Christ is and what He has done. After reading such a soul-stirring story of redeeming love, we bow before Him in adoration and worship. What a wonderful Savior is Jesus our Lord!

John: Glorify Your God

The Good News according to John is that Jesus Christ, the Savior of mankind, is God. Beginning with the truth of the eternality of the Holy Trinity, John reveals the glory of Christ in His incarnation, His deeds, His words, His atoning death, and His mighty resurrection. The writer, with unsurpassed clarity of expression, convincingly proves that Jesus Christ is very God of very God and very man of very man. He is "absolute, total God, the very God living in a human body."[48]

This eyewitness of the glory of God unhesitatingly declares: "The Word became flesh and lived for a while among us. We have seen his glory, the glory of the one and only Son, who came from the Father, full of grace and truth" (1:14 NIV).

The Gospel of John has been called the

most loved book in the Bible. . . . It has brought more inquirers into fellowship with Christ, it has led more believers into loyal service, it has raised and answered more questions in philosophy and religion than any other book.[49]

INFORMATIONAL MATERIAL

This Gospel is written by an inspired apostle who designates himself as "the one Jesus loved." Four times this expression is used: 13:23; 19:26; 20:2; 21:20. John cannot get away from the fact that he is an object of Christ's love. This "son of thunder," ready to call fire down from heaven (9:54) is utterly captivated by this love. Christ's love supernaturally transforms him from the inside out and makes him an apostle of love. Only the Godman can change such a rugged, fiery Galilean fisherman into a loving, sparkling, shining saint.

The shortest verse in the Bible is found here (11:35).

The content of the Gospel of John is structured to a large extent on geographical location and a chronological framework provided by a sequence of the various Jewish feasts. Therefore, when reading John, we should pay close attention to the places where Jesus is, what He says in that place, and to whom He says it. This is an important key in understanding the book. Jesus makes five visits to Jerusalem (2:13; 5:1; 7:2, 10; 10:22; 12:1, 12).

John writes with a purpose in mind—an evangelistic purpose (20:30–31). His compassionate heart longs for others to be saved and to experience this love. Consequently he writes to encourage faith in Jesus Christ. He uses the word "believe" again and again (ninety-eight times). John is saying, "Believe Him. Believe Him. Believe Him." In believing Jesus Christ, we have eternal life. We will never perish. Our body will certainly die, but our redeemed spirits will leap into the presence of God, and we will be forever with Him.

John makes clear what he writes. Often he makes a statement and follows it with an explanation. He wants the reader to know precisely what he says in order that there is no question about it (2:19–22).

This Gospel tells us that Jesus is very time conscious. Note the following expressions found in 2:4; 4:21; 5:25, 28; 7:6, 8, 30; 8:20; 12:23, 27; 13:1; 17:1.

There are a number of "I am" statements in John's Gospel. Jesus is the "Great I Am"; the bread of life (6:48); the light of the world (8:12); the door of the sheep (10:9); the good shepherd (10:11); the resurrection and the life (11:25); the way, the truth, and the life (14:6); the true vine (15:1).

This is the Christ John proclaims. He beheld His glory (1:14).

The glory

is constantly used either to designate all the attributes of the Godhead . . . or to indicate the manifestations of any one or of several of these attributes. Thus "his glory" may designate the radiance of the infinite love that dwelt in Christ, breaking forth again and again in word and deed; the heavenliness of his grace, or his mercy, or his compassion; the divine depth and comprehension of his wisdom and knowledge, against which also all human cunning failed; the absoluteness of his power in all the miracles that spoke so plainly of his divinity.[50]

"We beheld His glory" (1:14).

ANALYTICAL OVERVIEW

I. Prologue (1:1–18)
    A. The deity of Christ (1:1–13)
    B. The humanity of Christ (1:14–18)
II. The beginning of Christ's ministry (1:19–2:25)

A. His ministry to individuals (1:19–51)
B. His first miracle (2:1–12)
C. His visit to Jerusalem (2:13–25)
III. The effectiveness of Christ's ministry (3:1–11:57)
A. Dealing with individuals (3:1–5:18)
B. Speaking to the public (5:19–10:42)
C. Raising Lazarus from the dead (11:1–57)
IV. The last week of Christ's ministry (12:1–20:31)
A. His teachings (12:1–16:33)
B. His high priestly prayer (17:1–26)
C. His arrest, trial, crucifixion, and burial (18:1–19:42)
D. His resurrection from the dead (20:1–31)
V. Epilogue (21:1–25)
A. The manifestation of Christ to His disciples (21:1–23)
B. The witness of John for Christ (21:24–25)

PRACTICAL ASPECTS

Be prepared to suffer for doing right things. After doing right things such as teaching, loving, praying, even raising the dead, Jesus is arrested and crucified. Doing right things does not save us from suffering. Doing right things and suffering for doing them makes us Christlike, developing a Christlike nature within us. Always do the right thing. After the mightiest workings of Christ, there is still unbelief manifested—the unbelievers call a meeting of the Sanhedrin to destroy Jesus (11:47).

Because our Lord suffers undeservingly from those who reject Him, we too will encounter hardness and harshness from the unbelieving. Do not be surprised when it comes. God is getting us ready for something special.

It is necessary to keep in mind the cost of being Christ's followers. The other side of this truth is glory, blessing, and unspeakable joy—the joy of continuous growth in grace and fresh visitations of the Holy Spirit. The promise of Jesus to Nathanael is a case in point: "You shall see greater things than these" (1:50 NASB). The initial coming of Christ into our hearts is never to be considered an end in itself, but rather as the beginning of special spiritual realities to be experienced.

The longer and the further we go into the life of faith in Jesus Christ, the better and brighter the way becomes. "The path of the righteous is like the first gleam of dawn, shining ever brighter till the full light of day" (Prov. 4:18 NIV).

Conversion to Christ is not an endpoint, but only the beginning of a blessed life that really never ends. Even death does not bring it to an abrupt halt; it only transfers us from earth to heaven in a blaze of eternal glory.

Acts: Communicate Your Christ

F resh from the Mount of Olives where they have witnessed the thrilling sight of Jesus' ascension into heaven, the disciples return to Jerusalem to await the coming of the Holy Spirit. On that memorable day of Pentecost when the believers "were all together in one place" (2:1), the Holy Spirit comes "suddenly with a sound like the blowing of a violent wind" (2:2 NIV), filling each one with Himself. From this moment on, the Church of Jesus Christ witnesses to the gospel, communicating its message to those in Jerusalem, then onto Judea and Samaria, and ultimately to Rome—"to the ends of the earth" (1:8).

Acts is the exciting story of the Holy Spirit in dynamic action, working in the lives of Spirit-filled men and women, winning the lost to Christ and guiding the church in the ways of Christ. The Great Commission is being carried out literally as the church is on the move preaching, teaching, and baptizing. Luke's last statement tells of Paul in Rome, who "preached the kingdom of God and taught about the Lord Jesus Christ" (28:31 NIV).

Informational Material

The human author of Acts is Luke, who is an eyewitness of the many events about which he wrote. There are a number of "we" sections in the book proving this important point (16:10–17; 20:5–15; 21:1–18; 27:1–28:16). "These sections may read like leaves from a personal diary."[51]

Luke is the only Gentile writer included in the Bible. The Lukan books have been described as magnificent literature. They contain more content material than any other writings of a single author. The literary qualities, the composition, style, and other elements of his works are on a high level indeed. His writings reflect his appreciation of beauty.

As an author, Luke is careful and articulate, precise in researching details that he has checked and rechecked. Scholars have considered

> him among the best historians of his time. His literary ability is abundantly demonstrated by the Gospel and Acts, which are written in the finest Greek in the New Testament. His artistic nature can be seen in his arrangement of material and in the way he develops and presents his theme. His devotion to Jesus Christ is never obscured.[52]

Sir William Ramsay spent many years in research to check the accuracy of Luke. In becoming acquainted with detail after detail, fact after fact, he concludes that Luke is correct in his statements, reflecting the conditions of the first century.[53]

The purpose in writing the Acts is fourfold according to Rackham: (1) to convey accurate information in order that the reader might be grounded in truth; (2) to emphasize the important ministry of the Holy Spirit; (3) to trace the history of the Church from its origin to its establishment; and (4) to disclose the kind of human instrumentality the Holy Spirit used to extend the Kingdom of God.[54]

The dynamic action observed in the book is comparable to that found in the Book of Joshua. God's people are on the move. They are alive, aggressive, and alert. They are going places and doing things for God in the power of the Spirit. Their hearts are warm and glowing. They are aflame with the indwelling Christ. This book stirs us, excites us, and challenges us!

A thirty year period of time is covered by the book— 29/30A.D. to 60 A.D. The movement of the gospel goes from Jew to Gentile, from Jerusalem to Antioch to Rome.

ANALYTICAL OVERVIEW

I. Christ proclaimed in Jerusalem (1:1–8:3)
    A. The divine directives (1:1–11)
    B. The response of the disciples (1:12–26)
    C. The coming of the Holy Spirit (2:1–47)
    D. The ministry of Peter and John (3:1–4:31)
    E. The growth of the church (4:32–6:7)
    F. The ministry of Stephen (6:8–8:3)
II. Christ proclaimed in Judea, Samaria, and Antioch (8:4–12:25)
    A. The ministry of Philip (8:4–40)
    B. The conversion of Paul (9:1–31)
    C. The ministry of Peter (9:32–12:25)
III. Christ proclaimed in the Roman Empire (13:1–28:31)
    A. The first missionary journey (13:1–14:28)
    B. The conference in Jerusalem (15:1–35)

C. The second missionary journey (15:36–18:22)
D. The third missionary journey (18:23–21:16)
E. Paul's arrest and defense (21:17–26:32)
F. The journey to Rome (27:1–28:31)

PRACTICAL ASPECTS

Disciples may be taught over a dining table: "On one occasion, while he was eating with them, he gave them" a command (1:4 NIV). This is another one of Christ's post-resurrection appearances. He is in His glorified state, eating with His own. There is nothing carnal about this. I was taught that eating with Christians in a fellowship gathering such as this was not spiritual. When you meet with Christians, you are always to pray. This was difficult for me to unlearn. Now I seek to conform my life and ministry to the correct practices of Christ.

The Lord does not give a simple formula, outline a specific strategy, or reveal a secret code on how to be baptized with the Holy Spirit. He simply says, "Do not leave Jerusalem, but wait for the gift my Father promised" (1:4 NIV). He says in so many words: Obey Me. Remain in Jerusalem.

God always prepares His servant for His service. Paul is a classic example. Immediately after his conversion, Paul is not made a leader of the church, being thrust to the forefront. He is in Damascus witnessing, but then he goes into the desert of Arabia for some time. Three years after his conversion, he goes to Jerusalem for fifteen days (Gal. 1:18). The church leaders do not "grab onto him," giving leadership responsibility; rather, they take him to Caesarea and send him to Tarsus, his hometown (9:30). He is in Tarsus probably for seven to eight years, during which time he drops out of sight. Barnabas looks for him in Tarsus. Having found him, he brings him into Antioch (11:25–26). Both Barnabas and Saul teach great numbers of people. After teaching for a year in the church, both are called by the Holy Spirit (13:2). God seasons Paul over the years (eleven or twelve years) before He commissions him. *A call to service is a call to preparation!* God does not require a famous football quarterback nor a glamorous Miss America to further His cause and kingdom.

The words "gospel" and "good news" have the word *go* in them. Is this not significant? *Go with the gospel. Go with the good news.* The primitive church does—they go with it everywhere until Paul is able to make the following statement in the Colossian epistle: "The gospel . . . has been proclaimed to every creature under heaven" (Col. 1:23 NIV). This gospel is for the whole world—*go with it.* The early church goes from Jerusalem to Antioch, to Rome, to Europe, to Africa, and to India. The gospel has a worldwide reach.

Sin may be committed in the most unlikely places, at the most unlikely times, and by the most unlikely people. In the glorious hour when God the Holy Spirit is working mightily, Ananias and Sapphira lie to the Holy Spirit. Their judgment is immediate and causes great fear to seize the whole church (5:1–10). Do not let your guard down after great victories.

Growth of the body of Christ produces problems. This is normal when more people are involved in the work of the Lord. The primitive church has its problems; however, the Holy Spirit always has a solution. In the days when Grecian Jews complain against the Aramaic-speaking community, the apostles take the following steps (6:1–7): (1) they face their problem; (2) they call the believers together;

(3) they put the problem in proper perspective (the apostles will put the ministry of the Word first); (4) they let the believers make some choices; (5) they pray for those who are to be involved in the solution. Thus we have a problem-solving technique given us in this incident.

The Book of Acts reveals that God has a variety of ways in guiding us (e.g., [1] through an opportunity to serve [16:3]; [2] the check of the Holy Spirit [16:6–7]; [3] a vision from the Lord [16:9–10]; [4] the invitation of a convert [16:15]; [5] the action of the church [15:22]; [6] the command of God [13:2]).

Underscore the words *Holy Spirit* and *Jesus Christ while you read Acts.* By the power of the Holy Spirit, communicate Jesus Christ wherever you go.

Romans: Internalize Your Doctrine

The epistle to the Romans presents us with a comprehensive view of Christianity—its teachings and practices supported by biblical, historical validity. It has been rightly called "The Constitution of Christianity." To G. Campbell Morgan, Romans is considered one of the greatest writings of the New Testament. Martin Luther refers to it as the chief part of the New Testament and the perfect Gospel. Godet calls it "the cathedral of Christian faith."[55]

Romans is a trustworthy point of reference for faith, giving us a good beginning on an unshakable foundation. It is the authentic standard of inspired truth by which all Christian theology and living must be measured. It is the stationary North Star to guide us as believing pilgrims on our way home.

In Romans, Paul declares the essence of Christianity. He calls it the gospel. It is promised through the prophets in the holy Scripture (1:2). It centers in the Person of Jesus Christ—His death and resurrection (1:3–4). It reveals that God in Christ has provided righteousness for the sinfulness of mankind and that it is available to all who believe (1:16). "The righteous shall live by faith" (1:17).

The gospel is life-changing, sin-shattering, and hope-engendering. This is the Epistle of Romans.

INFORMATIONAL MATERIAL

The initial beginning of the Roman church is obscure. A reasonable suggestion is that those residents of the city who attended the Feast of Pentecost in Jerusalem witnessed the coming of the Holy Spirit. Returning to Rome, they give testimony to the gospel, thus planting a church (Acts 2:10). Should this assumption be true, the Roman church is among the oldest of New Testament churches. This indicates that at the time of Paul's writing, it is an established assembly, familiar with the gospel.

The church is composed of both Jew and Gentile believers. Because both groups are dealt with specifically throughout the epistle, it may suggest that Paul is building a bridge of meaningful relationships between them, teaching that God is no respecter of persons. Every believer, whether Jew or Gentile, has a part in the divine plan.

Paul is thankful for this church and prays for it (1:8–10). He desires to visit it and makes plans to do so (1:13). Because these plans do not materialize, he is led to write to them explaining his situation; but, more than this, to present in an orderly, logical manner the cardinal truths of the gospel.

The epistle contains many Old Testament quotations, indicating that Paul is indeed knowledgeable in Old Testament Scripture. He has been trained in it from youth. The many references he uses reveal what a well-read, well-informed, well-rounded scholar he is. The books from which

Paul quotes are as follows: Habakkuk, Psalms, Proverbs, Isaiah, Ezekiel, Ecclesiastes, Genesis, Exodus, Deuteronomy, Malachi, Hosea, Leviticus, Joel, 1 Kings, Job, and 2 Samuel.

The gospel has deep roots in Old Testament Scripture. These rich truths serve as strong meat for mature believers and pure milk for the young in faith.

ANALYTICAL OVERVIEW

I. Introduction (1:1–17)
II. Doctrinal (1:18–8:39)
    A. Condemnation of sin (1:18–3:20)
    B. Justification by faith (3:21–5:21)
    C. Identification with Christ (6:1–8:39)
III. Historical (9:1–11:36)
    A. Election of Israel (9:1–33)
    B. Gospel for Israel (10:1–21)
    C. Restoration of Israel (11:1–36)
IV. Practical (12:1–15:13)
    A. Spiritual responsibilities (12:1–8)
    B. Interpersonal relationships (12:9–13:14)
    C. Behavioral attitudes (14:1–15:13)
V. Personal (15:14–16:23)
    A. Paul's testimony (15:14–21)
    B. Paul's plans (15:22–33)
    C. Paul's greetings (16:1–23)
VI. Benediction (16:25–27)

PRACTICAL ASPECTS

Giving quality time for Bible reading enhances your knowledge of God. Moved with awe and wonder of Him, we become aware of His majesty, might, and magnificence. Paul says it so well: "Oh, the depth of the riches of the wisdom and knowledge of God! How unsearchable His judgments, and His paths beyond tracing out" (11:33).

How great God is, infinitely higher and greater than mankind. We are but dust. He makes the dust and out of it fashions man. We come into this world; He is already here. He is Creator; we are created. God owes us nothing; we owe Him everything, and even everything we may be allowed to have is His anyway. How great He is!

It is vitally important not only to know biblical truth but also to internalize it. The absolutes of the Word of God, including Romans, must pierce and permeate our innermost being until they become an essential part of us, giving us convictions of righteousness and holiness (6:1–23). Thus we not only hold convictions, but also convictions hold us.

Behind the Book of Romans lies years of earnest praying: "I have been longing for many years to see you" (15:23). With this longing Paul declares, "Constantly I remember you in my prayers at all times" (1:9–10). God answers those prayers in a most unexpected and unusual manner. In God's time Paul arrives in Rome as a prisoner (Acts 28:16).

When we pray submissively in the will of God, we do not know how the answer will be granted. We have a perfect scenario of the answer, but it does not always work out that way. We like to think of it as a neat package, tied with colorful ribbon—just exactly as we prayed. God does not always do things according to our way of thinking and planning, but in His time, in His way, according to His perfect will, He answers our prayers. Keep on praying!

The Epistle to the Romans is a presentation of the gospel—the good news that centers in Jesus Christ, His death and resurrection. The gospel is for lost humanity. It tells us what we are by nature—sinners. It tells us what we need—salvation. It tells us how God's provision in Jesus Christ meets that need. Therefore, regardless of how good a man may think he is or how bad he may be, he is always the prime object of God's grace—salvation. Paul makes this very clear in the opening chapters of the epistle.

The logical conclusion to the above statements is that to be an effective witness for Jesus Christ, we must keep in close touch with Romans. These are eternal truths relevant for every generation, not relative concepts subject to the whims and fancies of the worldly-minded. They are "true truths" as the late Francis Schaeffer referred to the Scripture.

Paul sets before us a shining example worthy of emulating. As a man of purpose, he lives and ministers with a goal in mind—that of proclaiming Christ where He is not known. He says it in these words: "It has always been my ambition . . ." (15:20). This divine "I must" is the driving force of his service for the Master. For Paul this is top priority.

What is your ambition? Remember: "Only one life, 'twill soon be past; only what's done for Christ will last."

1 Corinthians:
Correct Your Course

First Corinthians is like the ground-control center for the speeding space shuttle. It has many functions, including observations and making corrections. It is responsible for the shuttle staying on course. Paul writes 1 Corinthians in order to keep the church heading in the right direction—heavenward.

As he observes the church closely, he sees that it needs to correct its course. It is deviating and this could be disastrous. Therefore he appeals to the church to be united because it is off target with its dissensions. It needs to discipline the person guilty of immorality. It must not allow brother to go against brother in lawsuits before worldly tribunals. The church itself is to settle disputes and problems among believers. Moreover, moral purity is required of the body, which is a temple of the Holy Spirit.

In addition to making these corrections, Paul gives the church some practical and theological teachings on a variety of concerns expressed through their previous communications. By correcting and instructing the believers, he guides the people of God aright. This is 1 Corinthians.

INFORMATIONAL MATERIAL

According to Acts 18, Paul is the founding father of the church in Corinth, a pagan city known for its abominable vices. Farrar calls it, "The Vanity Fair of the Roman Empire."[56] He observes that the word "Corinthian" is a synonym for profligacy. In this place immorality and drunkenness are rampant. Certainly Corinth is "sin city."

How Paul comes to this stronghold of iniquity is a remarkable story in itself—the account of divine providence in the life of one who is fully committed to his Master. Step by step the Lord leads him, sometimes through supernatural means such as a vision, then again through opposition that causes him to go to another place. There are times when He leads him through brothers in the faith, who protect him and conduct him to a city such as Athens. Again, by his own decision before the Lord, he sets out for another field of ministry—Corinth.

God chooses this sin-soaked society for the purpose of rescuing it through the preaching of the cross by the apostle and thus changes lives into sparkling, shining saints. Paul arrives in Corinth a total stranger. After making an acquaintance with Aquila and Priscilla, tentmakers or workers in leather, he joins them in their occupation. On Sabbath days he preaches in the synagogue. Sometime later, he is aided by his coworkers, Silas and Timothy, who come to him from Macedonia.

Because of intense opposition, Paul moves his preaching activity from the synagogue to a nearby house. Here many respond to the Word of God and are converted. In a vision during the night, he is assured by his Lord that he is in His will and that he should continue his ministry in Corinth. He remains here for eighteen months.

During this extended period, the Corinthian believers become special to Paul. He loves them dearly. This fellowship of love continues over the years and is reflected throughout the epistle.

ANALYTICAL OVERVIEW

I. Introduction (1:1–9)
  A. Greetings (1:1–3)
  B. Thanksgiving (1:4–9)
II. Exhortations to the Corinthians (1:10–6:20)
  A. End your divisiveness (1:10–4:21)
  B. Discipline the immoral person (5:1–13)
  C. Stop your lawsuits against one another (6:1–11)
  D. Keep your body pure (6:12–20)
III. Instructions for the Corinthians (7:1–16:9)
  A. Concerning marriage (7:1–40)
  B. Concerning things sacrificed to idols (8:1–13)
  C. Concerning Christian liberty (9:1–11:1)
  D. Concerning worship (11:2–34)
  E. Concerning spiritual gifts (12:1–14:40)
  F. Concerning the resurrection (15:1–58)
  G. Concerning the collection (16:1–9)
IV. Conclusion (16:10–24)
  A. Final exhortations (16:10–18)
  B. Final greetings (16:19–24)

PRACTICAL ASPECTS

With wisdom of the Spirit, compassion of Christ, and commonsense tact, Paul deals effectively with the serious problems and transgressions of the Corinthian church. His epistle is a masterpiece of practical and theological teachings on dealing with Christians who are deviating from the ways of the Lord. His methodology is a wonder to behold and emulate.

At the very outset of the epistle, he establishes common ground on which to build a personal relationship with God's people. Paul is truly thankful for them, reminding them of their position in Christ. This thoughtful approach keeps doors of communication open. Throughout the epistle he continues to make the point clear of what true believers have in Jesus Christ. This not only gains their attention but also keeps it.

In dealing with authentic Christians with problems, we too should realize what they are in Christ. They have a position that is all of grace.

Having established rapport, at least in a measure, and also because he is their spiritual father, Paul calls attention to certain harmful practices not in keeping with a believer's position in Christ. This relationship should never be used for an excuse to downsize ethical and moral living. Their practices must be in keeping with biblical principles.

Therefore Paul calls attention to their shortcomings and sins; their problems, causing them to stray from the ways of the Lord. He does not skip lightly over the transgressions of the Corinthians. They must face up to them and do something about them, taking the proper actions he prescribes. They are to correct their course and "get with it."

We too should never gloss over sin. Let us face it; get rid of it; and keep going forward and growing in grace, making sure our practice is always in keeping with our position.

2 Corinthians:
Be Your Best

While Paul's first epistle to the Corinthians deals with directives for correcting various problems, the second urges the church to do still better. There yet remain certain areas of need that should come under the Lordship of Jesus Christ; specifically of the minority group led by false teachers, claiming official status, who challenge the apostolic authority of Paul.

Additionally the church is to cleanse itself "from all defilement of the flesh and spirit, perfecting holiness in the fear of God" (7:1). Believers are new creations in Christ, a people of God, separate from the world, set apart to Him Who redeemed them. Though they live in a wicked world, they are not of it. They are to think and act in this light, continually aiming to be their best for Christ.

What Paul says so effectively is, "Away with shoddy living in the flesh. Let there be an end to the party spirit, that air of superiority. 'Examine yourselves' (13:1). Be what God wants you to be, your best for Him."

Informational Material

In 2 Corinthians, Paul lays bare his heart to his readers in a manner unlike he does in any other epistle. His emotion is strong; his logic, deep; and his love, constant. This is a follow-up letter of a spiritual father who cares for his children of faith.

From the content of the epistle, Lias gives a fitting description of the writer:

> Human weakness, spiritual strength, the deepest tenderness of affection, wounded feeling, sternness, irony, rebuke, impassioned self-vindication, humility, a just self-respect, zeal for the welfare of the weak and suffering, as well as for the progress of the Church of Christ, and for the spiritual advancement of its members, are all displayed by turns in the course of his appeal, and are bound together by the golden cord of an absolute self-renunciation dictated by love to God and man.[57]

Paul has a threefold purpose for writing this epistle: to enlighten the church on the plans and principles of action of the apostolic ministry, which is to prepare the way for his return to Corinth; to appeal to the church regarding its Christian obligation to assist the poor with a generous offering; and to confront the critics, who are leveling false charges against him.

The epistle opens on a point of common interest: suffering and consolation (1:1–11). It closes with a benediction often repeated in the contemporary church (13:14).

Analytical Overview

I. Introduction (1:1–11)

A. Salutation (1:1–2)
B. Consolation (1:3–11)
II. Paul's purposeful minimessages (1:12–7:16)
   A. Personal plans and good intentions (1:12–24)
   B. Love and forgiveness (2:1–11)
   C. Old and new covenants (2:12–3:18)
   D. Human frailty and God's power (4:1–15)
   E. Hope and immortality (4:16–5:10)
   F. Fear and love (5:11–21)
   G. Mission and exhortations (6:1–7:4)
   H. Sorrow and rejoicing (7:5–16)
III. Paul's appeal for the offering (8:1–9:15)
   A. The example of the Macedonian churches (8:1–15)
   B. Arrangements for the offering (8:16–9:5)
   C. Principles of giving (9:6–15)
IV. Paul's defense against the critics (10:1–13:10)
   A. Consistency (10:1–11)
   B. Holy ambitions (10:12–18)
   C. Past and present experiences (11:1–33)
   D. Christ's revelation and power (12:1–13)
   E. Pastoral concern (12:14–21)
   F. Truthfulness (13:1–10)
V. Conclusion (13:11–14)
   A. Exhortations (13:11–13)
   B. Benediction (13:14)

PRACTICAL ASPECTS

Paul's experience of unspeakable glory of being caught up into paradise is followed by a *skolops*, a pointed stake, a thorn or splinter in his flesh (12:1–10). This penetrating irritation prompts him to pray earnestly three times for its removal. God answers his prayer with the promise of sufficient grace and power for his weakness.

The positive response of Paul is one of acceptance and even contentment because he knows this will keep him from self-exaltation and ultimate ruin. The *skolops* is used by God to accomplish a divine purpose in his life, to keep him completely dependent on Him.

Is not this one reason out of many why God allows the *skolops* in our lives: to activate us spiritually and to keep us going His way? Read on.

> The natives who fish off the coast of Maine go out to sea for weeks at a time to fish for herring. They keep the herring in a large box that floats in the water behind the boat.
>
> Fisherman Joe always brought his fish to market as fresh as the day they were caught. Yet his fellow fishermen brought herring to market that showed telltale signs of the weeks they had spent in the box at sea. Joe always commanded high prices for his herring, and for years the natives tried to find the secret of his success. Finally they were able to discover it.
>
> Fisherman Joe tossed his herring into the box just like all the others, but Joe always threw a catfish into his crate along with the herring. The catfish would chase the herring all around the box, keeping them lively and fresh. Perhaps the catfish would even eat one or two herring, but the remainder would increase in value because they were kept on the go. The catfish furnished the incentive for the herring to sustain their best physical condition.[58]

May the experience of Paul with the *skolops* and the illustration from marine life help to clarify things for us in those tough irritating times. Let us always remember: God is too wise to make a mistake and too good to do us harm!

Galatians: Maintain Your Freedom

While writing to the Galatian churches, Paul makes much of the gospel of Jesus Christ, the greatest message in all the world. There is no other like it.

Well did Bishop Kennedy of the Methodist Church say it in *Newsweek* some years ago: "We are not to think of the gospel as a book of home remedies. On the contrary, it is headline stuff, somebody yelling, 'Extra! Something has happened! Something tremendous! Better stop and hear what it is!'"[59]

It is this gospel that Paul proclaims once again to the Galatians in order that they might be delivered from the troubling influence of false teachers, who insist on keeping the law. They are attempting to bring the Christian under Jewish legalism.

Paul applies gospel truths in this situation, explaining once again that a person is justified by faith, not by the works of the law. Jesus Christ has made His people free, and they must maintain that freedom with holy living—living in the Spirit.

INFORMATIONAL MATERIAL

On one of his missionary journeys, Paul founds the Galatian churches. Out of a pagan environment, the Holy Spirit brings into being new creations in Jesus Christ. They welcome Paul as an angel of God or as Christ Jesus Himself (4:14).

After Paul leaves the churches, some Judaizers from Jerusalem come to these young converts and teach things contrary to the gospel. Evidently the false teachers are very impressive. They gain a following. This prompts Paul to write the epistle.

In contrast to the teaching of the Judaizers, Paul explains, in an elaborate argument, that the authentic gospel makes possible freedom from the Jewish practices of observing "days and months and seasons and years" (4:10) and circumcision (5:6; 6:12–13). Therefore is his epistle rightly called "The Magna Charta of Christian Liberty."[60]

This epistle has an authoritative tone. Paul is deeply moved as he writes. He does not give them the "kid glove," "velvet touch" treatment. His love is tough. He seeks to correct his spiritual children and to lead them in the right way—the way of New Testament gospel truth.

He shows no patience with the false teachers, condemning them severely (1:8–9), for they are hurting the cause of Christ. God's people are in danger, and Paul seeks to rescue them from spiritual disaster. He puts in sharp focus the difference between truth and error, faith and the law, and freedom and license.

While he warns of the perils confronting the believers, he seeks to win them for Christ, using expressions of kindness (1:3), concern (4:19–20), and confidence (5:10). Like a loyal warrior in battle, Paul fights the good fight of faith for God's people.

ANALYTICAL OVERVIEW

I. Introduction (1:1–5)
  - A. Paul's apostleship (1:1–2)
  - B. Paul's greeting and doxology (1:3–5)

II. Paul's message: the gospel (1:6–2:21)
  - A. Only one authentic gospel (1:7–10)
  - B. Christ revealed it (1:11–24)
  - C. Jerusalem church certified it (2:1–10)
  - D. The rebuke of Peter attested it (2:11–21)

III. Paul's message explained: the persuasion (3:1–4:31)
  - A. The Galatians' experience (3:1–6)
  - B. The faith of Abraham (3:7–14)
  - C. The promise of God (3:15–18)
  - D. The purpose of the law (3:19–25)
  - E. The illustration of an heir (3:26–4:7)
  - F. The recall of the past (4:8–20)
  - G. The allegory of the bondwoman and free woman (4:21–31)

IV. Paul's message applied: the exhortation (5:1–6:10)
  - A. Stand fast in Christ's freedom (5:1–12)
  - B. Do not take unwarranted liberties (5:13–15)
  - C. Walk by the Spirit (5:16–26)
  - D. Help one another (6:1–10)

V. Conclusion (6:11–18)
  - A. Glorying in Christ (6:11–14)
  - B. Final exhortations (6:15–17)
  - C. Benediction (6:18)

Practical Aspects

We will gain insight into Paul's attitude while writing the epistle if we will think of ourselves as one of the Galatian believers. We recall his message. We believe it. We receive Christ. We are saved.

Sometime afterward Jewish teachers, professing to be Christians, come to Galatia. They catch our attention. Their teaching seems logical. It does not conform to what we heard from Paul, our spiritual father, however. Without evaluating carefully and praying earnestly, we are tempted to accept this religious teaching because others in the churches have.

We begin asking questions. We discover that these men are berating Paul and denying his apostleship. This makes us hesitant to commit ourselves. While in this state of doubt and fear, our church receives a letter from Paul.

Do we see now why he writes as he does? Is he not rightly indignant? Does he not care for us and have our best interests at heart? Certainly he is giving us the truth. He writes as a faithful father. We respond positively to what he says. We reject the false teachers and with joy continue in the liberty of the gospel.

In speaking of joy, I am reminded of a mistaken notion I had during my youthful years, before I became a Christian. I hesitated to become one because I felt that all my joys in life would be gone forever should I make this decision. How wrong I was. I received Jesus Christ as my Savior and Lord, and He gave me what I thought I could never have—the *joy* of His salvation.

This is gospel freedom. I define it as "blessed bondage," which is as free as a train on its tracks. It is free to go all over the country, wherever the rails are laid. Having Christ choose the way for me is my joy. This freedom is super, for it ultimately leads to glory.

Ephesians: Acknowledge Your Creator

While chained to a Roman prison guard, Paul writes this epistle to the Ephesians and to all who are in the body of Christ. In those difficult days, he is given access to heaven. God opens up the gates of glory and gives him a glimpse of the splendor of divine activities relating to believers—the church.

With insight into the heavenlies, Paul becomes knowledgeable of what God did before the foundation of the world and what He planned for believers in every generation. Indeed, Ephesians begins on a high note. Paul is overwhelmed; therefore, he writes with "controlled ecstasy."

The Ephesian letter tells us that there is a divine side to the church. It is not of human origin; it is conceived in heaven, originating with God Himself. The church is God's idea, not man's; therefore, acknowledge and worship your Creator. Christianity is unique. It is not just another one of the world's religions. It is truly otherworldly with an earthly mission.

Putting the above in descriptive language, the church is on the drawing boards in eternity. God plans it. Jesus Christ carries it out in history; and through the ministry of the

Holy Spirit in today's world, the church is very much in evidence.

This is what Paul is telling us as he reveals doctrinal and practical truths to the church.

INFORMATIONAL MATERIALS

One of the Seven Wonders of the Ancient World is the gigantic temple in Ephesus where the pagan goddess Diana is worshiped. This draws large crowds far and wide throughout all Asia. It is the popular religion of the day.

Ephesus is also known for its magical arts and philosophers. This cosmopolitan city teems with a population of over 300,000 during Paul's day. Because of its strategic location, it is an important center for trade; hence, it is wealthy and prosperous.

Ephesus needs Jesus Christ desperately. Unafraid and unashamed, Paul takes the gospel to this city. His bold preaching in the synagogue is rejected after three months. This does not end his evangelistic outreach, for he goes to the lecture hall of Tyrannus and teaches there daily. So amazing are the results that he continues his ministry in that place for two years and more.

The impact of the preaching of the gospel is powerful. Extraordinary miracles are performed. Religious impostors are proved false. The silversmiths who are making shrines of Artemis are losing business because people are forsaking idolatry. Intense opposition is raised against Paul, but God protects him. Leaving Ephesus, he goes to another field, but not before a strong church is established and all Asia hears the Word.

The Ephesian church is a dynamic testimony to the trustworthiness of Jesus Christ's word: "I will build My Church" (Matt. 16:19). This He does in Satan's stronghold. Since the church is planned in heaven, there is no earthly or satanic power that can wipe it out. Christ's Church is worldwide in its scope, energized by the Holy Spirit, and protected by Almighty God because it belongs to Him. This is the unique body of Christ.

ANALYTICAL OVERVIEW

I. Introduction (1:1–2)
   A. The writer (1:1)
   B. The salutation (1:2)
II. Doctrine: the Church planned by God in heaven (1:3–3:21)
   A. Conceived before the foundation of the world (1:3–4)
   B. Executed through Christ (1:5–12)
   C. Sealed with the Spirit (1:13–14)
   D. Enlightened through prayer (1:15–23)
   E. Created in Christ (2:1–10)
   F. Built for God's presence (2:11–22)
   G. Blessed through grace (3:1–13)
   H. Strengthened through prayer (3:14–21)
III. Practice: the Church exhorted by God on earth (4:1–6:20)
   A. Walk worthy (4:1–6)
   B. Serve faithfully (4:7–13)
   C. Mature spiritually (4:14–16)
   D. Live godly (4:17–5:14)
   E. Walk carefully (5:15–21)
   F. Interact respectfully (5:22–6:9)

PRACTICAL ASPECTS

Since the church is of divine origin, God intends that it be established as a dynamic presence for righteousness in a pagan society. It is to be a deterrent to evil. Its mission is clear and costly, often misunderstood by those whose lifestyle is just the opposite. It is not to catch the spirit of the age, but to conquer and overcome it.

Paul says it forcibly when he declares that a Christian is to be done with the old life in his new life in Jesus Christ. He should seek to live in conformity to God's will. This is why Paul devotes half of his letter to the practical side of Christianity only after laying the groundwork of sound doctrine.

These principles of conduct are given to converted Gentiles who have had no religious background as did the Jewish believers. Paul expects both to conduct themselves in a Christlike manner, making no difference between them. There are not two standards for Christians. Both are exhorted to walk with God, whether their background is pagan or religious, and both are to shine for Christ in a dark world.

Paul's emphasis on the Christian home reveals the importance of maintaining and cultivating good family relationships. Strong families make for strong churches and also for a strong nation. As the home goes, so goes the nation. The strength of the nation is in the homes of its people.

Jesus Christ is to be preeminent in our lives. When He is, we discover that we have a battle on our hands—one against Satan. Therefore, in concluding his letter, Paul tells us to put on the full armor of God in order that we may stand firm "against the schemes of the devil" (6:10–20). And pray!

How good Ephesians is for us in our times.

Philippians: Share Your Joy

O f all the Pauline epistles, Philippians is the most
personal one written to a congregation. Tenney observes
that approximately one hundred times Paul uses the first personal pronoun, not in the sense of boasting, but because of
his close relationship to the Philippian church.[61] This is Paul's
"sweetheart" church, and he expresses himself freely to her.

In the difficult circumstances of imprisonment, Paul is
positive and praiseful as he writes. His epistle is an expression of joy in the Lord because of the grace granted him. He
is not living under his circumstances, being overwhelmed
by them; rather, he is living with Jesus Christ in them.

Rightly does Lenski comment, "Joy is the music that
runs through this epistle, the sunshine that spreads over all
of it. The whole epistle radiates joy and happiness."[62]

To those "singing the blues," Paul's words are like those
of a father putting his hands on his son's shoulders and
saying, "I love you. I am with you. I want you to know that
in your darkest hours, Jesus will not fail you. You can always depend on Him. Live for Him wholeheartedly."

This is the Philippian epistle—joyful assurance in Christ;
the Sovereign God is in control; and Christians have responsibilities to carry out.

INFORMATIONAL MATERIAL

Paul plants his first church on European soil in Philippi, the leading city of Macedonia (Acts 16). The gospel continues its westward thrust and ultimately reaches America. Paul is assisted by Silas, Timothy, and Luke.

From an inconspicuous beginning, the church develops into a strong congregation of believers. Paul's point of contact is with a group of praying women who meet by the riverside outside the city. The witness of the gospel is given to a businesswoman named Lydia, whose heart the Lord opens to respond to the truth. Not only does she become a believer, but her entire household also trusts Jesus Christ as Savior. They follow the Lord in water baptism.

While ministering in Philippi, Paul and his coworkers are confronted by a demon-possessed slave girl, who brings much profit to her masters by fortunetelling. By the power of God the demon is cast out of her. Since these evil men can no longer make profit from her, they vent their wrath against Paul and Silas by dragging them before the Roman authorities.

After beating God's servants, they throw them into prison. Paul and Silas pray and sing during the midnight hour. God is so pleased with their songs and prayers that He sends an earthquake. The jailer, becoming distraught and fearful, is ready to take his life. Being restrained by Paul, who tells him how to be saved, the jailer believes on Jesus Christ. He and his household are baptized that very night.

This is the background of the church in Philippi. Now, about ten years later, Paul writes this joyful epistle to them. He who sang in the jail in Philippi continues his praise in the Roman prison as he writes to the church. His exhortation is: "Rejoice!" He practices what he preaches.

ANALYTICAL OVERVIEW

I. Introduction (1:1–11)
    A. Salutation (1:1–2)
    B. Thanksgiving and prayer (1:3–11)
II. The report from the Roman prison (1:12–26)
    A. Results of the imprisonment (1:12–18)
    B. Personal desires expressed (1:19–26)
III. The exhortation to godliness (1:27–2:18)
    A. Conduct yourselves in a worthy manner (1:27–30)
    B. Be Christlike in your attitude (2:1–11)
    C. Continue in obedience (2:12–18)
IV. The affirmation of God's servants (2:19–30)
    A. Timothy (2:19–24)
    B. Epaphroditus (2:25–30)
V. The personal witness to Christ (3:1–16)
    A. Paul's life before conversion (3:1–7)
    B. Paul's life after conversion (3:8–16)
VI. The second series of exhortations (3:17–4:9)
    A. Follow Paul's example (3:17–4:1)
    B. Live in harmony (4:2–3)
    C. Rejoice and pray (4:4–7)
    D. Obey God (4:8–9)
VII. The expression of gratitude (4:10–20)
    A. Words of appreciation (4:10–17)
    B. Needs abundantly supplied (4:18–20)
VIII. Conclusion (4:21–23)
    A. Final greetings (4:21–22)
    B. Benediction (4:23)

PRACTICAL ASPECTS

Out of the prison in Rome come words of encouragement from one of its inmates—a saint of God held there for his fearless faith in Jesus Christ: "Being confident of this, that he who began a good work in you will carry it on to completion until the day of Christ Jesus" (1:6 NIV).

Paul is in Philippi when God begins His gracious work in the hearts of the believers years before. He remembers so well, and now he tells them that the Lord is going to complete His work. What God begins, He always finishes. He does not stop in the middle of the process of His plan. He keeps on doing what He knows to do so well until the day of Jesus Christ.

This is to say that the child of God can be assured the Holy Spirit will continue His working until the very end. There will be times when it seems that nothing is happening, a dry period is experienced, the storm hits, the bottom drops out, the outlook is bleak; but this does not mean that God ceases His workings, even though we feel pain and pressure. Does He not promise to finish what He starts? Let Him do it.

Listen to this prisoner as he continues his epistle: "But I press on to take hold of that for which Christ Jesus took hold of me" (3:12 NIV). This is Paul going forward in the divine purpose for his life while he is confined in chains, believing God has so much more for him. In his heart he continues striving for the prize ahead. It is God Who is always at work in him unto the very end.

May this too be the driving force in our lives—to go forward in each trying time in life. This attitude, coupled with praise, is a winning combination.

There have been times in my life when I felt that God was silent. With a burdened heart, I got down on my knees and said to Him, "Lord, I am going through with You regardless of how I feel." In His time and way, the battle was won; therefore, I have learned to always keep pressing ahead with praise. This is the victory.

Colossians: Unburden Your Heart

Pastoral cares may at times become a heavy burden and a cause for deep concerns. What does a pastor do when his heart is overwhelmed? He turns to the Lord first of all; and then, like Epaphras, he may seek help from a fellow servant of Christ.

The Colossian epistle tells of a pastor's contact with the apostle Paul. Epaphras makes a special trip to Rome to consult with him about church matters. Paul listens intently while Epaphras pours out his heart and tells of the faith and love that abounds in the church. He is troubled about some problems arising among the people, however. False teachings are beginning to show their ugly heads—deceptive philosophy, legalism, mysticism, and asceticism.

Upon hearing these concerns, Paul goes to prayer, asking God to fill the believers with a knowledge of His will, to enable them to walk worthy of the Lord, to increase their knowledge, and to strengthen them with His power (1:9–11). It is apparent that God answers his prayer, and shortly thereafter Paul writes the epistle. It touches those very areas of Epaphras' concerns and the things for which Paul prays.

The implication of all this is that an epistle of lasting value comes into being because one man of God unburdens his heart to another man of God. Consequently significant things take place. The church in Colossae is enlightened, and the unburdened heart finds relief and refreshment.

INFORMATIONAL MATERIAL

The destination of this epistle is the church located in Colossae, a city approximately one hundred miles east of Ephesus in Asia Minor, now known as Turkey. There is no record of Paul's personal visit to the church. Usually he writes to those he had ministered to previously. Now while being held as a prisoner in Rome, he pens the Colossian epistle.

Paul carries on a ministry for nearly three years in Ephesus with great effectiveness some five or seven years before his imprisonment. Acts tells us that all who live in Asia hear the word of the Lord. God performs extraordinary miracles through him (Acts 19:10–12). The results are amazing and far reaching.

Scripture does not tell us how the people in Asia are reached with the gospel. A church is planted in Colossae, however, and Epaphras serves as pastor, no doubt its founding father.

The Colossian letter mentions Epaphras several times (1:7–8; 4:12–13). Paul highly regards him as a beloved fellow bond servant, a faithful minister, and a fervent "prayer," who is filled with deep concern for the church.

The doctrine Paul writes of is Christocentric and practical. The Christlike life is to be evidenced in everyday, consistent conduct. Moreover, the epistle is polemic in nature as it deals with problems and their solution. Paul gives a masterful argument in warning of the dangers of false teaching confronting the church.

Well does Erdman observe:

> He corrects error by the forceful presentation of truth. He does not emphasize the heresy or advertise the heretics. He gives, instead, a matchless presentation of the all-sufficiency of the person and work of Christ.[63]

ANALYTICAL OVERVIEW

I. Introduction (1:1–14)
    A. Salutation (1:1–2)
    B. Thanksgiving (1:3–8)
    C. Prayer (1:9–14)
II. The person and work of Christ (1:15–23)
    A. His deity (1:15–17)
    B. His headship (1:18)
    C. His sacrifice (1:19–23)
III. The message and ministry of Paul (1:24–2:5)
    A. Christ-centered (1:24–27)
    B. Purposeful concern (1:28–2:5)
IV. The warning and argumentation against error (2:6–23)
    A. Vain philosophy (2:6–12)
    B. Religious legalism (2:13–17)
    C. Intellectual mysticism (2:18–19)
    D. Humanistic asceticism (2:20–23)
V. The instructions and exhortations for Christlike living (3:1–4:6)
    A. Seek the things above (3:1–4)
    B. Put off the old life (3:5–11)

    C. Put on the new life (3:12–17)
    D. Nurture family life (3:18–4:1)
    E. Carry out spiritual responsibilities (4:2–6)
 VI. Conclusion (4:7–18)
    A. Personnel report (4:7–17)
    B. Personal greetings (4:18)

PRACTICAL ASPECTS

We cannot read this epistle without becoming aware of the splendor and glory of Jesus Christ. How great He is! He is the visible representation of the invisible God in Whom all fullness of Deity abides, being Creator, Preserver, Redeemer, and Head of the Church, which is His body. He is before all things—eternal. He has no equal.

He, through His supreme sacrifice on the cross, pouring out His life's blood, makes possible the forgiveness of sins and the hope of eternal glory, saving from the uttermost to the uttermost.

Not only has Jesus Christ done great things for us because of Who He is, but He desires to do great things *in* us. Christ is to be internalized in our lives—our thinking, our speaking, and our doing. We are to live in Him, and He is to live in us, for He is our Head. From Him we receive our supply for all of our needs and our directions for the way we are to go. We are not our own; we belong to Him.

Drink daily from this Fountain of Life. Partake of this Bread from heaven. In so doing, we will find Jesus Christ to be precious indeed; adequate for struggles, problems, and temptations; and a Friend Who sticks closer than a brother.

1 Thessalonians:
Expand Your Horizons

The epistle addressed to the Thessalonians is among Paul's first and, therefore, one of the oldest of his New Testament writings. It is sent to a newly planted church—authentic believers who are living in the warmth of first love for their Lord. Both believing Jews and Gentiles comprise the congregation.

In order to catch the meaning of this epistle, it is suggested that the reader think of being a new or recent convert. Remember when your life was transformed by the power of the gospel. You were never again the same. This was the case of the Thessalonians.

As we read the epistle with this thought in mind, we readily see why Paul writes as he does. The young converts need love, support, and assurance. Paul reveals his tender love for them, his genuine concern, his earnest longing to see them, and his deep desire to help them. They are precious and important to Paul—and to Christ and His kingdom, as is every newborn in the faith.

Informational Material

Luke, the beloved physician and historian, tells of the founding of the Thessalonian church in Acts 17:1–9. Intense opposition is raised against Paul and the believers. This young church experiences suffering and persecution. Paul alludes to this in his epistle.

The apostle comes to Macedonia because of a night vision of a man who says, "Come over to Macedonia and help us" (Acts 16:9 NASB). Immediately Paul responds and sets sail for his new field of service. After planting a church in Philippi, he goes to Thessalonica, the second largest city of the district with a population of approximately 200,000.

Paul's point of contact in the city is a Jewish synagogue where he preaches on three successive Sabbaths. The thrust of his message is the death and resurrection of Jesus Christ. There is an immediate response by some Jews, a large number of God-fearing Gentiles, and not a few prominent women (Acts 17:4).

An avalanche of opposition and persecution falls on God's people, making it difficult to follow Christ. Nevertheless, they continue to receive the Word with the joy of the Holy Spirit. In this environment of adversity, a church is brought into being. What a testimony to the power of the gospel.

The purpose of the epistle is to comfort and to challenge young believers. Paul gives them the precise truths they need for their times.

Analytical Overview

I. Salutation (1:1)
II. Personal: a review of the past (1:2–4:12)

A. The believer's experiences (1:2–10)
B. Paul's ministry (2:1–16)
C. Timothy's visit (2:17–3:10)
D. Paul's exhortations and instructions (3:11–4:12)
III. Prophetical: a preview of the future (4:13–5:11)
A. The hope of believers (4:13–15)
B. The coming of Christ (4:16–5:3)
C. The call to alertness (5:4–11)
IV. Practical: a high view of the present (5:12–27)
A. Exhortations to holy living (5:12–22)
B. Expectations for holy living (5:23–27)
V. Benediction (5:28)

PRACTICAL ASPECTS

Little does Paul know how greatly God will use him in Macedonia. The facts are now clear: Churches are planted in Philippi, Thessalonica, and Berea. Epistles are addressed to two of the congregations; these survive the test of time and come down to us. The lesson is obvious: The individual who obeys the call of God will have a vital ministry. He may never realize how great it is while he lives; its scope may be even greater after he dies.

This epistle abounds with evidences of authentic Christianity—faith, hope, and love. Watch for these words as you read the epistle. Faith produces good works. Love motivates untiring labor. Hope inspires steadfastness. May these excellent qualities increase and abound in your life.

In proving his love for this young church, Paul uses three figures of speech. The first is that of a nursing mother (2:7); the second, a caring father (2:11); and the third, a hurting orphan (2:17). The New International Version translation speaks of him as "being torn away" from them. Actually the participle Paul uses to describe his deep feelings is a word in the original language meaning "to make an orphan of someone."[64]

He longs to be with them, but being separated from them makes him feel as if he is orphaned.

The Second Coming of our Lord is mentioned in each chapter (1:10; 2:19; 3:3; 4:13; 5:2). Every believer will be drawn to Jesus Christ when He returns. This suggests something of the sweetness and comfort of His coming—our blessed hope.

It is necessary for the Christian to read the Word daily, because the writer tells us that when it is received it works in us (2:13). The Holy Spirit uses God's Word to convict, to convert, to change, to cleanse, to comfort, and to challenge us.

Paul's letter teaches us truth concerning the sovereignty of God. He is in absolute control of the universe. There are times when this does not seem to be the case; nevertheless, He rules even though we may not understand what He is doing.

The apostle experiences testing times too. He tells of his desire to return to Thessalonica, but Satan hinders him. The New International Version puts it: "Satan stopped us" (2:18). What does a believer do when this happens? Look to your Sovereign Lord, because He opens other doors leading to a greater ministry. He does this for Paul, and He will do it for us.

God is Sovereign. He Himself says, "I am the Lord, and there is no other" (Isa. 45:6 NIV). He will always have the last word. Believe Him. Expand your horizons. Always keep the big picture in mind.

2 Thessalonians:
Keep Your Balance

When we are under the pressure of intense sufferings and erroneous opinions, we face the danger of losing our sense of spiritual balance. We are tempted to take fanciful and fanatical positions. We become extremists. Such is the case of some of the Thessalonians.

This young church is in need of divine guidance. Paul, their spiritual father, responds to these problems immediately; therefore, he writes the second letter to them.

The problems are twofold: one, a mistaken view of Christ's coming (2:3); the other, a foolish notion that working is no longer necessary (3:10). Some in the congregation are becoming lazy.

To keep the church moving in the right direction, Paul writes this epistle.

INFORMATIONAL MATERIAL

It is important to keep in mind that this epistle is written to young converts who are zealous for their Lord. Paul is supportive of them. He writes of his thankfulness for them (1:3) and continues to pray for them (1:11).

The apostle's teaching on the Second Coming profoundly affects the believers. They expect Christ immediately. Paul tells them that the time for His coming will not take place until the man of sin is revealed. Before Christ comes there will be lawlessness and apostasy. The Lord will judge both the antichrist and all who are identified with him (2:3–10). This has not yet taken place.

The Second Coming of Christ is the climactic event of human history. It is to be thought of in two distinct aspects: One is that He will come to meet His people in the *air* (1 Thess. 4:13–18). We call this the rapture. The other is when He comes, He will be revealed on *earth* (2 Thess. 2:3–8). This is the revelation.

We discover in both epistles that Paul puts emphasis on working—by example (1 Thess. 2:9) and by exhortation (2 Thess. 3:9–15). Thus does he rebuke laziness as well as declare a Christian work ethic.

Be assured Christ is coming; wait for Him and while you are waiting, work!

ANALYTICAL OVERVIEW

I. Salutation (1:1–2)
II. Personal: words of encouragement (1:3–12)
    A. Thanksgiving (1:3–4)
    B. Encouragement (1:5–10)
    C. Prayer (1:11–12)
III. Prophetical: words of enlightenment (2:1–17)
    A. The call to steadfastness (2:1–2)
    B. The coming of antichrist and his destruction (2:3–12)
    C. The consolation of the chosen (2:13–17)

IV. Practical: words of exhortation (3:1–15)
    A. Pray (3:1–5)
    B. Work (3:6–10)
    C. Obey (3:11–15)
V. Benediction (3:16–18)

PRACTICAL ASPECTS

Let me once again suggest a profitable exercise in the reading of Paul's epistle: Visualize yourself as a young convert in the Thessalonian congregation. In so doing, you gain greater insight into its meaning and significance. Some word or sentence arouses your attention.

When Paul's name is mentioned at the very first, fond memories of his ministry no doubt fill the minds of the believers. Recalling his dynamic ministry is so refreshing, just as you are blessed when you receive a word from your spiritual father. You are "all ears." You receive the word with joy; so did the Thessalonians.

As a sponge soaks up water, so the young church absorbs the truths from the apostle's pen. That word enlightens, comforts, and penetrates their hearts.

Paul, at the very outset, gives them words of assurance. He declares that the church is being built on a solid foundation. It is "in God our Father and the Lord Jesus Christ" (1:1). The Father and the Son bring the church into being by the Spirit of God and the Word of God. It has deep roots in deity. The Lord is in the believers and believers are in Him. What blessedness!

In continuing his letter, Paul lets the church know that in God's time everything is going to be all right (1:6–10). They may be suffering now, but the day is coming when all this will change. God is a righteous judge. He will vindicate His people, and He will punish the wicked—those who have caused suffering to His people. Certainly truths such as these lift sagging spirits.

Once more Paul touches on the theme of the Second Coming of Christ, giving details he did not disclose in the first epistle. God's people must be reminded again and again of the blessed hope. This teaching serves as an incentive for holy living and honest working.

The problems that need attention are handled adequately and forthrightly by Paul. May God enable each of us to be helpful and tactful in ministering to people with problems. While we live in a topsy-turvy world of turmoil and trouble, deception and deterioration, looseness and laziness, let us continue in the Word and keep looking for Christ's coming.

Maintain your balance!

1 Timothy:
Guard Your Trust

Biblical truth is indeed a rare jewel, a precious commodity —more precious than gold; therefore, it must be guarded with a faith that will not falter in the face of opposition, persecution, or ridicule.

The martyrs of the past ages give positive testimony to their love of the truth by laying down their lives for it. They are burned at the stake, put in dank dungeons, and placed in iron chains. Unflinchingly these custodians of the faith guard it well, even to the very end.

Biblical truth is an absolute, not a variable; eternal, not temporal. It is this kind of truth Paul imparts to Timothy, passing it on to a fellow believer like a runner in a relay race. Timothy is to hold on to it, practice it, and entrust it to others. This epistle, addressed to him personally, has to do with his placement—what he is to teach; how he should select leaders for the church and relate to others; and that he himself should live a disciplined life. The truth is given to him to keep, to practice, to use, and to proclaim.

In addition, 1 Timothy, along with 2 Timothy and Titus, known as the pastoral Epistles, are guidelines for pastors in their leadership role in the church.

Informational Material

"In the year 1726, Paul Anton wrote a book on the letters to Timothy and Titus, using the designation 'Pastoral Epistles.' The name has gained such currency that no other is likely to displace it . . ."[65]

This epistle written by Paul is addressed to Timothy, a young pastor, who serves the church in Ephesus. His hometown is Lystra in what is now called Turkey. Born of a Jewish mother and Greek father, he is taught the Scriptures from his childhood. Having been brought to faith in Jesus Christ through the ministry of Paul on his first missionary journey, he is asked to join the evangelistic party several years later.

Timothy remains an esteemed fellow minister with the apostle, sharing also in Paul's persecutions. His dedicated life is acknowledged by Paul, who refers to him as "a man of God" (1 Tim. 6:11).

Unfortunately, Timothy has gotten bad press from some scholars who have used isolated biblical passages to portray him as fearful, timid, and sickly. I cannot agree with this. The full picture of Timothy's life must be considered. Over the years he is Paul's companion in rigorous missionary endeavors. Certainly no one who is not courageous, or who backs away from persecution and hardship, could keep in step with Paul. Timothy doggedly seeks to carry out each directive from his leader. I see Timothy as strong and brave; otherwise, Paul would not have asked him to continue pastoring in Ephesus, the pagan capital of idolatry. No weakling could serve in this capacity.

It is to be remembered that while this epistle is addressed to one person, its truths are for the church—all Christians, clergy and laymen alike.

ANALYTICAL OVERVIEW

I. Salutation (1:1–2)
  A. The writer (1:1)
  B. The addressee (1:2*a*)
  C. The greeting (1:2*b*)
II. The task assigned to Timothy (1:3–20)
  A. Teach sound doctrine (1:3–11)
  B. Consider Paul's testimony (1:12–17)
  C. Keep the faith (1:18–20)
III. The responsibilities of laity (2:1–15)
  A. Duties of men (2:1–7)
  B. Duties of women (2:8–15)
IV. The qualifications for church leaders (3:1–16)
  A. For bishops (3:1–7)
  B. For deacons (3:8–16)
V. Personal directives for Timothy (4:1–6:10)
  A. Receive the enlightenment of the Spirit (4:1–5)
  B. Discipline yourself (4:6–16)
  C. Be sensitive to interpersonal relationships (5:1–2)
  D. Give assistance to widows (5:3–16)
  E. Honor the elders (5:17–25)
  F. Teach godly principles (6:1–10)
VI. Paul's final charge to Timothy (6:11–21*a*)
  A. Be true to God (6:11–16)
  B. Instruct the rich (6:17–19)
  C. Guard your trust (6:20–21*a*)
VII. Benediction (6:21*b*)

PRACTICAL ASPECTS

One of the implications of this epistle is that our Lord has a special interest in young people and He invests heavily in them. They are important to Him. Timothy is one of these; for early in life, he receives the riches of God's grace, which pay handsome dividends of many years of devoted and untiring service in His cause.

In looking at the sacred record, many are the young people the Lord puts His hand on. There is young Mary, a pure virgin, who is chosen to be the mother of Jesus Christ, God's beloved Son.

Through years of preparation, young Joseph is raised up by God to become the prime minister of Egypt. A young shepherd boy named David becomes king over Israel. In a pagan government, young Daniel is taken from the status of a slave to that of an official in the king's court. Young Queen Esther is used to save her people from destruction.

All of this proves that God loves young people and desires them for Himself. They are precious to Him. Throughout the generations, this has always been evident.

Let God make His investment in you, and, by all means, guard that trust with your very life!

2 Timothy:
Perform Your Mission

The last words of a dying Christian hold special significance. When a loved one is about to depart from this life, we listen intently. We do not want to miss a single spoken word. We are all ears.

This reminds me of the day Mother and I visited my Father in the hospital. Shortly after arriving in the room, we heard him talking. He was saying, "There's a river. There's the tree . . . and angels. You ought to get a picture of that."

As I listened, I wondered if Dad was going to die immediately or if he knew what he was saying. My Sister came into the room a little later. Recognizing her presence, Dad said, "I'm so glad you came, Lucille. I felt a little while ago I was going to be with Jesus. But I didn't go after all. I guess He is going to make my journey a little longer. Not my will, but His be done. The Lord will take care of you."

The next evening Dad went into the presence of his Savior. I will always cherish those last words. They are full of faith and hope. How blessed to die in Christ—to be with Him.

Paul's last written words are the Second Epistle to Timothy. How precious they are. Read them with confidence. They will bless, guide, search, and encourage you.

INFORMATIONAL MATERIAL

One of the important keys of understanding this epistle is to keep in mind that Timothy is not a novice starting out in the ministry; rather, he is a seasoned veteran, having served with Paul for a number of years. At the time of this writing, he has logged perhaps twelve or fifteen years in Christ's service.

From some of the evaluations made of Timothy, I do not think that this vital fact is taken into consideration; hence, an inferior image of him has been presented.

Imprisoned and awaiting trial in Rome, Paul writes 2 Timothy. While he faces the possibility of a martyr's death, he writes to one facing life; the aged apostle is concerned about the young pastor in Ephesus. Certainly there is no generation gap between these two men of God. Both are headed in the same direction—heaven.

While Paul is confident and full of hope, Timothy may be apprehensive, wondering what will happen to his spiritual father. Therefore the epistle is full of encouraging words and directives with regard to the course Timothy should take in carrying out his mission.

Also in this epistle there is an urgent request. Timothy is asked to come to Paul in Rome as soon as possible (4:9, 21). Whether or not he is able to be with him before his death, no one knows. Knowing Timothy's faithfulness, however, I am sure he made a gallant effort to be there.

ANALYTICAL OVERVIEW

I. Introduction (1:1–5)
    A. Salutation (1:1–2)

B. Thanksgiving and prayer (1:3–5)
II. Paul's exhortations for Timothy's encouragement (1:6–18)
    A. Continue stirring up the gift of God (1:6–7)
    B. Join in suffering for the gospel (1:8–12)
    C. Be true to your trust (1:13–14)
    D. Keep in mind Onesiphorus (1:15–18)
III. Paul's exhortation for Timothy's development (2:1–4:8)
    A. Be strong in Christ's grace (2:1–13)
    B. Render service with diligence (2:14–21)
    C. Practice personal discipline (2:22–26)
    D. Be aware of the times (3:1–9)
    E. Continue in the things learned (3:10–17)
    F. Preach the Word (4:1–5)
    G. Follow Paul's example (4:6–8)
IV. Paul's personal reports (4:9–18)
    A. Concerning fellow ministers (4:9–13)
    B. Concerning Alexander the coppersmith (4:14–16)
    C. Concerning the Lord's faithfulness (4:17–18)
V. Conclusion (4:19–22)
    A. Final greetings (4:19–20)
    B. Request for Timothy to come to Rome (4:21)
    C. Benediction (4:22)

PRACTICAL ASPECTS

This epistle brings us face to face with the realities of death and life. Paul realizes his days on earth are limited. Looking ahead, he is ready to go to his Lord. He says to Timothy, "For I am already being poured out as a drink offering and the time of my departure has come" (4:6).

Readiness, or preparedness to die, should be the top priority of every Christian. All of us will someday experience death whether we feel like it now or not. Therefore, like Paul, fight the good fight, finish your course, and keep the faith (4:7). This is excellent preparation for what lies ahead—the death of the physical body.

But this is not the end—far from it. There is glory following—"the crown of righteousness" (4:8). And while we anticipate the future, we are to face the challenges of everyday living. This is what 2 Timothy teaches, for it gives us valuable insights on how to live and how to minister in our world. Indeed, walking in the light of this word will not only prepare us for living but also for dying. Thus, by God's grace, we will be enabled to say, "Mission accomplished."

Titus: Exercise Your Leadership

L et us call him Titus the Troubleshooter, the dynamic, fearless, outgoing coworker with Paul, an expert in the field of public relations. If we want a courageous man to implement a plan, to solve a difficult problem, call on one like Titus. His willingness to help in any situation is so refreshing that it almost sweeps us off our feet.

It is this man Titus, to whom Paul addresses his epistle, and who has his confidence and respect. Paul asks him to remain on the island of Crete where a number of churches are located. They are unorganized and in disarray. To complicate the problem, the churches are in an environment of a sinful society, whose inhabitants are "liars, evil brutes, lazy gluttons" (1:12 NIV).

Titus takes on Paul's assignment, having received the grace of God in salvation and being made of the stuff of spiritual manliness. With God's help, he will get the work done.

Paul gives him his orders to organize the churches, appoint spiritual leaders, minister to the men and women, the young and old, and thus lead them with firm love to a higher level of authentic Christian living. To do this, it is important that Titus exercise his leadership.

Informational Materials

The field of service to which Titus is assigned is Crete, a large island in the Mediterranean Sea, about 160 miles long, of unequal width, ranging from six to thirty-five miles. In ancient times, Crete had a fairly large population. Homer spoke of its hundred cities. Many of its people were sailors and archers.

It is not known how Christianity is planted here. The Book of Acts tells us that Cretans are present in Jerusalem on the day of the outpouring of the Holy Spirit (2:11). No doubt they carry the good news back to their people.

Over the years, serious problems develop in the churches, necessitating closer supervision of them. Paul asks Titus to become a problem solver at this time.

He is brought to Christ through Paul's ministry. Referring to him as "my true son" (1:4 NIV), Paul also calls him "my brother" (2 Cor. 2:13) and "my partner and fellow worker" (2 Cor. 8:23). After Titus helps to straighten things out in the Corinthian church, Paul is greatly encouraged and comforted by his report (2 Cor. 7:6, 7, 13). Titus is one to be trusted in complex situations.

With Paul and Titus, we have a blending of personalities in the fellowship and service of the Lord. Both are walking in the same spirit, on the same path, striving for the same goals.

Analytical Overview

I. Introduction (1:1–4)
   A. The writer (1:1–3)
   B. The addressee (1:4a)

C. The salutation (1:4*b*)
II. The purpose for Titus in Crete (1:5–16)
  A. To bring order in the churches (1:5*a*)
  B. To appoint qualified elders (1:5b–9)
  C. To silence the opposition (1:10–16)
III. The content of sound doctrinal teaching (2:1–3:11)
  A. The necessity of godliness (2:1–10)
  B. The manifestation of God's grace in Christ (2:11–15)
  C. The social responsibilities of Christians (3:1–3)
  D. The manifestation of God's saving work (3:4–11)
IV. Conclusion (3:12–15)
  A. Personal requests (3:12–14)
  B. Final greetings (3:15*a*)
  C. Benediction (3:15*b*)

PRACTICAL ASPECTS

Paul gives Titus two important exhortations concerning personal guidance as to his whereabouts. One is near the beginning of the epistle; the other at the end: "The reason I left you in Crete was that you might straighten out what was left unfinished . . ." (1:5*a* NIV) and "As soon as I send Artemas or Tychicus to you, do your best to come to me at Nicopolis . . ." (3:12*a* NIV).

Does not this suggest that in order for one to be guided aright he must be pliable, not rigid; always ready to stay or to go as the Lord leads? This requires a surrendered will of the servant to his Master, Who knows the time and place for the most effective service.

In matters of guidance God often leads us through a godly person as in the case of Paul with Titus. This is a valid principle, not necessarily spectacular or sensational. How often does our Lord lead us in "ordinary" ways rather than through extraordinary manifestations?

Therefore, it follows that we must be fully and absolutely surrendered to our Lord if we are to be in the place He wants us in His time.

Are you one of His committed servants? Pliable—like clay in the Potter's hands?

Philemon: Accept Your Prodigal

How well God knows that this world is full of prodigals —people estranged from Him because of their sinful living. Yet His love is continually reaching out to them. Jesus Himself tells us of the prodigal son, who, having come to himself, repents and returns to his father. He is welcomed home with joy.

In this epistle Paul writes about a prodigal slave, Onesimus, who is brought to Christ and becomes a new man. His empty and useless life is now made full and useful by the grace of God. Both Jesus and Paul teach us that God loves the prodigal and wants him for Himself.

INFORMATIONAL MATERIAL

Writing from his prison in Rome, Paul pens this brief, yet very important, epistle to Philemon, a resident in or near Colossae. It serves as a bridge of reconciliation between a master and his runaway slave.

Included in the addressees of the epistle are Apphia, perhaps the wife of Philemon, Archippus, and the house church. Apparently it is Paul's desire to have those who are knowledgeable of the circumstances surrounding Onesimus' disappearance to know that he has not only been found but is also soundly converted to Christ.

How Onesimus is brought in touch with Paul the prisoner no one knows. The apostle is deeply moved by the radically changed life of this new convert, who serves him faithfully. Should he have his way, he would keep Onesimus with him. Knowing Roman law, however, Paul realizes that he must be returned to Philemon.

This letter prepares the way for Philemon to receive Onesimus, no longer as a slave, but as a beloved brother. Paul's earnest plea to Philemon on behalf of Onesimus reveals his heart of compassion for young converts and his sensitivity for compliance with Roman law.

According to Colossians 4:7–9, we learn that Onesimus accompanies Tychicus in returning to Colossae. One can only imagine the time of rejoicing in the church when the prodigal slave comes home.

ANALYTICAL OVERVIEW

I. Introduction (1–3)
    A. The writer (1a)
    B. The addressees (1b–2)
    C. The salutation (3)
II. Paul's prayer for Philemon (4–7)
    A. Thankful prayer (4–5)
    B. Specific prayer (6–7)
III. Paul's plea for Onesimus (8–22)
    A. A courteous plea (8–11)
    B. A tactful plea (12–14)

C. A reasonable plea (15–17)
D. A responsible plea (18–20)
E. An anticipating plea (21–22)
IV. Conclusion (23–25)
    A. Final greetings (23–24)
    B. Benediction (25)

PRACTICAL ASPECTS

God be praised for the wonder of redeeming love. When Onesimus is running away from it all, he runs right into the arms of the Savior, Who forgives him and wipes out the old sinful record. Now he can be a blessing in his service for the Master in Colossae—all because of God's grace.

We don't have to be somebody special to receive His grace. It is freely given to everyone—the unknown, the little known, and the undeserving. God isn't looking for star performers, supermen, or headline personalities. All He wants is an open heart in which to deposit the riches of His grace. He is reaching out to us today. He assures us that a slave of sin, a prodigal, can become a beloved brother or sister in Christ.

Hebrews: Behold Your Savior

At the risk of sounding too simplistic, let me say it with all my heart: Jesus Christ is the answer. The writer to the Hebrew Christians declares it emphatically as he portrays Jesus Christ as our great high priest, seated at God's right hand, Who makes intercession for us. Because of Him our needs are met, our problems are solved, and our prayers are answered. Therefore we fix our eyes on Him. Behold your Savior!

The priests in Old Testament times fulfilled their responsibilities before God; their work is done. It is no longer necessary to depend on them and their religious system of worship.

God sends His beloved Son to take over the priestly responsibilities. Jesus Christ sheds His blood as the supreme sacrifice for sin and is raised to eternal glory, thus inaugurating the new covenant.

The Jewish believers have difficulties with this as they are influenced by those who desire to have them live under the old order. The writer of the epistle, through sharp contrasts, shows the difference between the old and the new way of life in Christ. He does this by revealing the exalted nature of the Son of God, by issuing warnings of the danger of reverting to the former ways, and by giving encouragements to believe God. Jesus Christ is Lord and Savior. Only in Him are we acceptable to God.

INFORMATIONAL MATERIAL

The author of this epistle is not known. Some suggest that Paul, Barnabas, Apollos, Silas, or Luke might have written it. Actually only God knows who did.

The writer is knowledgeable of the practices of Judaism. He knows the Old Testament well as he quotes from many of the books such as Psalms, 2 Samuel, Deuteronomy, Isaiah, Genesis, Exodus, Jeremiah, Habakkuk, Proverbs, and Haggai.

He knows the truths of the gospel that center in Jesus Christ, Who is superior to angels, Moses, and those of the Levitical priesthood. God has spoken in His Son (1:1–3), Whose greatness is unmatched, Whose power is unlimited, and Whose glory is unequaled.

The book contains words of encouragement as well as words of warning. Herein are many doctrinal and practical truths vividly illustrated. Attention is given to details. Even personal concerns are mentioned. Erdman observes that "it begins as an essay or treatise; it progresses as a sermon or homily; it ends as a letter."[66]

This epistle is addressed to Hebrew Christians with a background in the Old Testament and who are partakers of the gospel of Christ.

ANALYTICAL OVERVIEW

I. The deity of Christ (1:1–14)
    A. Equal with God (1:1–3)
    B. Superior to angels (1:4–7)
    C. Eternal in being (1:8–14)
    First warning: against negligence (2:1–4)
II. The humanity of Christ (2:5–3:6)

    A. Made lower than angels (2:5–9)
    B. Made in the likeness of men (2:10–18)
    C. Made superior to Moses (3:1–6)
    Second warning: against unbelief (3:7–4:13)
III. The ministry of Christ (4:14–10:18)
    A. Based on grace (4:14–16)
    B. Superior to Aaronic priesthood (5:1–4)
    C. Followed the order of Melchizedek (5:5–10)
    Third warning: against immaturity (5:11–6:12)
    D. Confirmed by God's oath (6:13–20)
    E. Greater than Levitical priesthood (7:1–25)
    F. Exalted in the heavens (7:26–8:5)
    G. Established with a better covenant (8:6–13)
    H. Surpassed Old Testament symbolism (9:1–11)
    I. Accomplished by the shedding of His blood (9:12–23)
    J. Continuing in heaven at God's right hand (9:24–28)
    K. Is of eternal efficacy (10:1–18)
IV. The sufficiency of Christ (10:19–12:29)
    A. To help those who come to Him (10:19–26)
    Fourth warning: against apostasy (10:27–31)
    B. To give victory to people of faith (10:32–12:2)
    C. For the discipline of His own (12:3–17)
    Fifth warning: against refusal (12:18–29)
V. Conclusion (13:1–25)
    A. Final exhortations (13:1–17)
    B. Personal considerations (13:18–25)

PRACTICAL ASPECTS

According to the analytical overview of the epistle, the writer gives five specific warnings. They are real danger signals to be taken seriously. Think of the second warning, which has to do with unbelief (3:7–4:13).

We must guard against this damaging sin, which is as deadly as a poisonous rattlesnake on a desert floor, ready to strike; as dangerous as the rotten wood covering a deep well; and as destructive as a smoking volcano, pouring its fiery stream against everything in its wake.

Remember what unbelief did for those on their way to the Promised Land. "They were not able to enter because of their unbelief" (3:19 NIV). Unbelief will keep us from enjoying God's best.

On the other hand, think of what faith in the Son of God will do. The writer devotes much of his message on the positive side—faith. The entire eleventh chapter gives a remarkable portrayal of those who believe God.

Take for example Noah.

> It was through his faith that Noah, on receiving God's warning of impending disaster, reverently constructed an ark to save his household. This action of faith condemned the unbelief of the rest of the world, and won for Noah the righteousness before God which follows such a faith (11:7 Phillips).

Noah fought the same kind of battle that we are in today—against doubt, fear, and unbelief. He acted on what God said, not on what he saw or felt. This we need to do also, for faith in the Word of God is the sure way to win in the struggles of life and to gain the victory. Keep your eyes on Jesus. Behold your Savoir!

James: Show Your Faith

This epistle is one of the earliest of the New Testament writings. Others will follow. It serves as a bridge for the people of God to make the transition from Old Testament times to the New Testament order. Step by step the change is made as James brings together the old with the new, which, when completed, forms an authoritative, infallible revelation of God—the Bible.

When James writes to the believers, the church is young, perhaps some twenty years old. It is composed largely of Jewish believers. It is only natural then to have this kind of an epistle addressed to them—one they can readily understand considering their religious background.

These Jewish believers have new life in Jesus Christ. They are no longer under the Old Testament order. They are to be top quality Christians. Therefore, James tells them in practical terms how they are to live. These are the basic guidelines for the spiritual development of the church of the twentieth century—also for you and for me.

INFORMATIONAL MATERIAL

James is the half-brother of Jesus Christ. How fitting that the Holy Spirit should select him to write the earliest book of the New Testament.

There is a time when James does not believe that Jesus Christ is the Messiah (John 7:5). The turning point comes in his life when the resurrected Lord appears to him (1 Cor. 15:7). From this time on James becomes His devoted follower. He is one of the participants in the upper room prayer meeting when the Holy Spirit comes to the believers on the day of Pentecost (Acts 1:14).

He emerges as a leader in the church; he presides over the first Jerusalem Council (Acts 15:13). He is deeply spiritual and highly respected. Tradition tells us that he has knees like those of a camel because he spends so much time in the temple praying.

Throughout the epistle we observe that James has a firm grip on Old Testament Scripture and New Testament thought as revealed by Jesus Christ. Like his Lord, James uses many illustrations from the realm of nature and also concepts Jesus gives in the Sermon on the Mount. His language is direct, concise, and simple. He has a high view of God and of Scripture. When we read what he says, we know what to do as a Christian.

James writes with compassion. He calls believers, "beloved brethren." He knows the trials of these who "are scattered among the nations" (1:1) because of their faith in the Lord. He appeals to them to be strong and not to give in to the adversaries with a "pity party," but to rejoice, to pray, to live consistently, and to be patient for the Lord is with them in the trying times.

ANALYTICAL OVERVIEW

I. Introduction (1:1)
II. Trials and temptations (1:2–18)
   A. The right attitude toward trials (1:2–8)
   B. The right attitude toward self (1:9–12)
   C. The right attitude toward God (1:13–18)
III. Hearing and doing (1:19–27)
   A. Receive the Word (1:19–21)
   B. Act on the Word (1:22–27)
IV. Favoritism and transgression (2:1–13)
   A. Favoritism illustrated (2:1–4)
   B. Favoritism forbidden (2:5–13)
V. Faith and works (2:14–26)
   A. Faith without works is meaningless (2:14–17)
   B. Faith without works is useless (2:18–20)
   C. Faith without works is lifeless (2:21–26)
VI. The tongue and talk (3:1–12)
   A. The tongue is powerful (3:1–6)
   B. The tongue is untamable (3:7–8)
   C. The tongue is deceitful (3:9–12)
VII. Wisdom and righteousness (3:13–18)
   A. True wisdom (3:13)
   B. False wisdom (3:14–16)
   C. Divine wisdom (3:17–18)
VIII. Strife and submission (4:1–10)
   A. The blight of strife (4:1–5)
   B. The blessing of submission (4:6–10)
IX. Speaking and judging (4:11–12)
   A. The command against evil speaking (4:11a)
   B. The reason for the command (14:11b–12)
X. Self and sovereignty (4:13–17)

    A. The assertion of self (4:13–14)
    B. The recognition of sovereignty (4:15)
    C. The application of Scripture (4:16–17)
XI. Riches and retribution (5:1–6)
    A. The distress of shortsightedness (5:1–3)
    B. The disapproval of selfishness (5:4)
    C. The defilement of sinfulness (5:5–6)
XII. Patience and prospect (5:7–11)
    A. The exhortation to patience (5:7–9)
    B. The examples of patience (5:10–11)
XIII. Practices and prayer (5:12–18)
    A. In living: be true to your word (5:12)
    B. In suffering: pray (5:13*a*)
    C. In joy: sing praises (5:13*b*)
    D. In sickness: seek God (5:14–18)
XIV. Conclusion (5:19–20)

PRACTICAL ASPECTS

Tests and temptations are the realities of life. There is a vast difference between the two. God tests us in order that we might be quality Christians. He puts us through various processes that reveal weaknesses, impurities, or any other deficiencies that require His working within us. In testing us, our Lord searches, corrects, cleanses, disciplines, and blesses us.

He tests our faith. For example, He may challenge us with a handicap, a hindrance, an emotional low—when feelings take wings and fly away. Our test: Will we continue to believe God even though we do not feel like it?

How well I remember when God tested me like this in one of my pastorates many years ago. In today's language, I was distressed, depressed, and felt terrible for quite some time. One day for our morning devotions, my wife and I read from *Streams in the Desert*. The emphasis of the devotional was on praise. For two solid weeks, without any special feeling, I praised the Lord. The victory and the blessing ultimately came. Out of that testing time the Lord taught me the lesson that I have been learning over the years: "The just shall live by faith." Are you depending on feelings, or are you living by faith?

On the other hand, a temptation is an enticement to do evil, to commit sin. God *never* leads us to sin. The pull toward sin is from our own sinful lusts (1:13–14) or from Satan who seeks to lead us astray.

God is totally good. He does not tempt, but He tests us. Make sure you have a handle on the difference between a test and a temptation. James helps us sort it all out.

1 Peter: Follow Your Shepherd

This epistle is written by Peter, who at one time vehemently opposed the idea of Christ's suffering and death but who comes to embrace wholeheartedly these important truths. Now he proclaims them unashamedly and forthrightly. To him, the death and resurrection of Christ are the cornerstone of sound theology and practice.

Throughout the epistle, Peter speaks of the suffering of the Savior—not incidentally but intentionally—and weaves into this magnificent fabric of divine truth the reality of the Christian's sufferings. They too are identified with their Lord—the Shepherd of their souls.

With tender compassion and sincere exhortations, Peter gives Christ's followers specific directives as to how to live in distressing times. His epistle is full of hope, encouragement, and consolation—for suffering is followed by glory. This is the saint's heritage in following their Shepherd.

INFORMATIONAL MATERIAL

While living in a land of spiritual darkness, Peter becomes one of the sons of light through the saving grace of the One Who is the Light of the world. He is introduced to Christ by his brother, Andrew.

The Master molds this Galilean fisherman into a spiritual leader and a gifted writer, who contributes two epistles to the New Testament. Peter leads an exciting life as he walks and talks with his Savior for many years.

Peter's educational experience is in Christ's school of experience. Today we would call it field education—a very effective means of producing realistic and knowledgeable ministers. Few people have been so blessed as Peter and the first apostles.

With a warm heart he writes this epistle. He is empathetic with those who are suffering for the Savior's sake. He too knows the cost of following Jesus. He seeks to strengthen faith and exhorts the believers to stand firm. At times he uses long sentences, indicating that he is a clear and logical thinker. He writes in excellent Greek. Even the scholars marvel at this. He holds before his addressees the living hope, based on the resurrection of Jesus Christ. In trying times, this hope serves as an anchor to the soul.

ANALYTICAL OVERVIEW

I. Introduction (1:1–2)

II. Spiritual relationships (1:3–2:12)
   A. Based on Christ's death and resurrection (1:3–12)
   B. Cultivated through faith and obedience (1:13–2:12)

III. Social relationships (2:13–25)
   A. With civil authorities (2:13–17)
   B. With masters (2:18–25)

IV. Marital relationships (3:1–7)
   A. The wife's responsibility (3:1–6)
   B. The husband's responsibility (3:7)

PRACTICAL ASPECTS

This epistle reminds us that Jesus Christ saves us for Himself, for His purpose, that we might be obedient to Him (1:2, 14, 22). Obedience to Him will not only bring blessing and strength, but guidance and protection. At times we discover that obedience is costly, especially when we do the right thing and, like Jesus, suffer for it.

Therefore, we are not to be surprised when this happens (4:12). Peter tells us what to do. Do good (2:15, 20). Rejoice (4:13), as Peter himself does (Acts 5:41). Do not be ashamed (4:16). Commit yourself to God, your faithful Creator (4:19) as the Savior Himself did (2:23). This is Christlike living.

The Lord uses the testing times in our lives to develop, enlarge, and strengthen our faith. We may not think so, especially if the trial is deeply distressing and long. Nevertheless, what we feel does not alter nor nullify God's eternal promises. He "is the same yesterday and today and forever" (Heb. 13:8). We live by faith in Him and His Word.

Peter tells us that there is a divine side to the believer, even though we sense the frailty of humanness. We are God's elect, having been chosen by Him (1:1). He draws us to Himself, selects us that we might declare the praises of Him Who called us out of darkness into His wonderful light (2:9).

Barclay uses the following illustrations to explain the meaning of the word "chosen." It describes specially chosen fruit. Articles are especially chosen because they are so outstandingly well made. Picked troops are especially chosen for some great duty or some great exploit.[67] The Lord selects us to be in a special relationship with Him. What an honor!

We who are the "called-out ones" are to live differently in the worldly environment in which we are placed. The pagan world thinks of us as being strange individuals because we do not engage in their debauchery and dissipation (4:2–4). We have been changed by the transforming power of the gospel, and our Savior has made us rejoice.

It is true as the songwriter once put it: "I lost the world and the world lost me, when I found pardon at Calvary." But the riches of love in Christ Jesus make up infinitely more than what we lost. Now ours is a life full of hope. This hope has to do with our final salvation—ultimate deliverance which is in readiness to be revealed (1:5). Therefore, continue following the Shepherd.

2 Peter: Increase Your Knowledge

An apostle of Jesus Christ is standing on the threshold of death; he will soon go from time into eternity. Just before he leaves this life, Peter has one last message for the church—his Second Epistle.

He writes with sincerity and urgency, seeking to stimulate believers to wholesome thinking (3:1). They are to grow in the grace and knowledge of their Lord and Savior Jesus Christ. They must not be satisfied with the status quo but add quality to their spiritual lives. They have a rock-solid foundation on which to build. Also, their faith is supported by historical evidence and fulfilled prophetic statements of the Old Testament.

Peter tells his readers that there are specific truths to accept, errors of false doctrine to reject, and realities of the future to anticipate, for which they should prepare. This message is a shaft of light on the pilgrim's pathway to eternal glory.

INFORMATIONAL MATERIAL

When Peter is a young, zealous follower of Jesus Christ, he is told the kind of death he would experience—

crucifixion (John 21:18–19). Now some thirty years later, he is nearing that point of martyrdom as he writes his last epistle, which is certainly inspired by the Holy Spirit and comes out of years of faithful service for his Lord.

Peter is now a man of maturity who knows firsthand the trials and triumphs of life. He is qualified to write as he does.

The apostle's concerns reach far beyond those of his own, for he has in mind the people of God who will remain after he is taken from them. It is his desire that they will always remember those truths in which they are firmly established (1:12; 3:1). Thus Peter is ministering to future generations—to you and to me.

This epistle also reflects Peter's knowledge of the Old Testament. He calls attention to significant historical events. He speaks of the sure words of the prophets, and he tells of a new heaven and a new earth as does Isaiah. He quotes from the Proverbs. This is evidence that he is familiar with the three divisions of the Old Testament—the Law, the Prophets, and the Psalms.

There is a marked difference of emphasis in Peter's two epistles. The first has to do with encouragement and hope for the suffering; the second, with the need for continuous growth in grace and knowledge. The growing Christian becomes stronger and wiser. He does not succumb to the pressures of false teachers. He is fruitful and effective!

ANALYTICAL OVERVIEW

    I. Introduction (1:1–2)
    II. Authentic truths (1:3–21)
       A. God's provision (1:3–4)
       B. Believer's growth (1:5–11)

Practical Aspects

It is through the increase of biblical knowledge that we grow in grace. Peter would have us know that there are vast areas of spiritual enrichment available to us and that we should lay claim to them. God's promises are given for this very end. These blessings become a reality to us when we take God at His Word. We receive by believing and acting upon them.

Do you desire a warm welcome into the eternal kingdom? If so, add the qualities of goodness, knowledge, self-control, perseverance, godliness, brotherly kindness, and love to your faith (1:5–9). These qualities will have a positive effect in your life. You will be an effective and fruitful Christian who is in the process of being prepared for eternity with Christ.

When Peter raises red flags of warning against false teachers, he lets us know that they are the subjects of God's intense wrath, as are all who identify with them. Our holy God cannot condone sin. He is righteous. (See chapter two.)

In matters of divine justice and judgment we must side with God.

The Sovereign Lord is also gracious and patient. He is not willing that any should perish but that all come to repentance (3:9). It is God's kindness that leads people to repentance (Rom. 2:4) and ultimately to glory.

What is your view of God? Is it in keeping with the truths found in this epistle?

1 John: Test Your Profession

Incredible—that God should take a Galilean fisherman, one of the "sons of thunder," and use him to become a writer of the Holy Scriptures; and not only of one book of the New Testament but five—the Gospel, three Epistles, and the Revelation!

But is not this like the Lord, to take a person we think is unqualified, transform him into a new creation, fill him with the Holy Spirit, and grace his life with supernatural gifts? John stands as a powerful testimony for all time to the work of God in a human heart.

No doubt John, now an older man—probably ranging in age from the eighties to the nineties—has been in touch with Christ for many years. Infected with the love and truth of the Savior, he spreads that glorious contagion everywhere throughout his world, reaching down to ours. Would God that every reader of this epistle experience the same blessedness!

In understandable language John stresses the practical side of Christianity, which has deep roots in doctrinal truths. He points out specific evidences of spiritual birth, using the expression "born of God" to describe them. When they are found in our lives, we can be assured that we are authentic Christians.

What John says in so many words is, "Test your profession. Are these evidences of the new birth seen in your life?" Note 2:29; 3:9; 4:7; 5:1, 4, 18. This is a book of assurance for the believer in Jesus Christ.

INFORMATIONAL MATERIAL

Although the author's name is not given in the epistle, it is quite evident from internal evidence that John, the apostle, is the writer. The prologue of 1 John, although much shorter, bears close resemblance to the prologue of the Gospel of John.

Also, like the Gospel, the language of the epistle is not complex but easy to read. The vocabulary of both books is similar, with such words as "light," "truth," "belief," "love," "abide," and "righteousness" being frequently used.

John does not write in long sentences. The issues he deals with are both theological and practical. In the epistle, he often uses contrasts, recognizing the great gulf between light and darkness, black and white, truth and error, sin and righteousness, love and hate, life and death, Christ and antichrist, children of God and children of the devil. With John there is no middle ground, no gray area, no twilight zone.

Without hesitation he calls sin, sin—not an alternative lifestyle, not a flaw, not a mistake, not a weakness, not a personality problem. John says that sin is lawlessness (3:4) and all unrighteousness (5:17). It can only be cleansed from the heart through confession and the blood of Jesus Christ (1:7–9).

For John, the vital truths of the gospel are not deep, dark, complicated secrets to be discovered by brilliant minds. They are simple and understandable words, coming from a heart of love. He calls his readers, "my little children" and "beloved."

In the epistle there are no quotations from the Old Testament, perhaps suggesting that John is writing for those believers who have come from a pagan background.

His purpose in writing is that all believers may have fellowship with Jesus Christ and with one another (1:3–4).

Tradition tells us that his field of ministry is Ephesus and perhaps in the surrounding area as an overseer of other churches since the center of gospel activity moves from Jerusalem and Antioch.

ANALYTICAL OVERVIEW

I. Prologue: the apostolic confession (1:1–4)
    A. The living word (1:1–2)
    B. The spoken word (1:3)
    C. The written word (1:4)
II. The authentic message (1:5–2:2)
    A. God's holiness (1:5–7)
    B. Man's sinfulness (1:8–10)
    C. Christ's righteousness (2:1–2)
III. The evidences of knowing God (2:3–3:20)
    A. Obedience (2:3–6)
    B. Love (2:7–11)
    C. Enlightenment (2:12–27)
    D. Hope (2:28–3:3)
    E. Righteousness (3:4–10)
    F. Consistency (3:11–20)
IV. The exhortations to the beloved (3:21–4:21)
    A. Keep the commandments (3:21–24)
    B. Test the spirits (4:1–6)
    C. Love one another (4:7–21)
V. The exercise of faith in Christ (5:1–17)

A. Transforms the believer (5:1–3)
B. Overcomes the world (5:4–8)
C. Receives assurance (5:9–12)
D. Engages in prayer (5:13–17)
VI. Conclusion (5:18–21)
A. Review of truths (5:18–20)
B. Final exhortation (5:21)

PRACTICAL ASPECTS

John, through the authority of the Holy Spirit, sets the ground rules for practical Christian living. These are not mere suggestions but commandments from our Lord Himself. In a word they are the fundamental principles guiding Christians in everyday living.

How unnecessary it is to shy away from the fundamentals. So many seem to be afraid of this important word. To some it sounds like an overload of rigidity, strictness, legalism. Therefore, we have a tendency to soften the commandments and fundamentals. We do it to the hurt of the cause of Christ, which results in an "anything goes," "don't fence me in," "I got to be me" attitude and slipshod, lackadaisical living.

Let us seek to meet the standard John raises. Does he not assure us that "His commandments are not burdensome" (5:3)? Remember the words of Jesus: "If you know these things, you are blessed if you do them" (John 13:17).

In the world of sports, the athlete must play according to the fundamentals and rules of the game, no matter how gifted or creative he may be. If he is inclined to do otherwise, he will be benched or receive his walking papers.

Should not the true Christian obey his Lord's commandments and fundamental principles to glorify Him?

2 John: Watch Your Step

Second John is a short but a significant sacred writing. It should not be passed over lightly. The Lord gives it to us for a purpose—for our good. It reveals the importance of abiding in love and truth, disclosing the vital relationship of the redeemed to sound doctrine, essential for a discerning spirit, enabling us to detect false doctrine and deceivers.

Love and experience alone are not enough because experience is a variable, whereas truth is an absolute. The Christian with the love of God in his heart must not only be closely connected to the Word of truth but also have that Word abiding within him always. Therefore, it does make a difference what a person believes regarding biblical doctrine.

This epistle teaches us that the person who does not abide in the teaching of Christ does not have God (9). Indeed, this strong statement is worthy of our attention and acceptance. Therefore watch your step as you walk with God. Walk in love and truth.

Informational Material

The writer refers to himself as the elder, without giving his name. Certainly the original addressees knew who this was. Even centuries later we recognize it, as did they, to be John the apostle, one evidence being that of the close relationship to 1 John. The concepts of love, truth, and warning against antichrist are prominent in both epistles.

The epistle is addressed to the chosen lady and her children. Some interpret these words as a literal distinguished Christian woman and her children. Others suggest that the chosen lady is a local church and her children are members of the congregation.

I prefer this latter view, because the teachings of the epistle seem to be intended for a larger group—a church congregation—rather than for a single family, a mother and her children.

The fatherly spirit of the author, who is deeply concerned for the people of God, indicates that this epistle comes from John, the disciple whom Jesus loves. Christian tradition supports Johannine authorship.

ANALYTICAL OVERVIEW

I. Introduction (1–3)
    A. The writer (1a)
    B. The addressees (1b–2)
    C. The salutation (3)
II. Exhortations (4–11)
    A. Walk in love (4–6)
    B. Watch for deceivers (7–11)
III. Conclusion (12–13)
    A. Personal hopes (12)
    B. Final greetings (13)

PRACTICAL ASPECTS

You have seen signs, when boarding a bus or walking on a slippery floor, urging caution. They may say, "Watch your step" or other words of warning.

Some pay little or no attention to danger signals. They throw caution to the winds. They are daredevils with the attitude of a macho man—afraid of nothing. This may sound big and strong, but the braggadocio is not exempt from a fall.

Every wise person will heed red flags. The Bible alerts us to pitfalls. This is why faith must feed on the Word of God daily; only then will it remain strong and discerning. Are you a daily reader of the Scriptures?

Second John sounds its danger signals against error and its consequences. God knows that human strength alone cannot ward off the deceptive tactics of the devil or of religious deceivers with a "peaches and cream" message. But through the Word of God and the Spirit of God, the discerning believer overcomes the foe.

Watch your step and walk with God.

3 John: Weigh Your Walk

D id you ever receive a brief note with these words at the top: "From the desk of," "Memo," or "A reminder"? No doubt many of you have. The brevity of the message does not detract from its importance. Similarly 3 John is like this—a concise epistle of significant truth, needing to be read by all Christians.

It is intensely personal, coming from the overflowing love of the writer to Gaius, whom he calls "beloved" (NASB) or "dear friend" (NIV). In his characteristic style of writing, John uses contrasts for emphasis, pointing out the difference between Gaius who is walking in truth and Diotrephes who is not.

How important it is for a Christian to walk in truth (3–4). Therefore let every person reading this epistle weigh his walk.

INFORMATIONAL MATERIAL

There are common threads of truth running through all three epistles of John, whether they be long or short. These are difficult to overlook. They point to a common authorship—that of John.

This epistle gives us a brief description of the three principal persons mentioned: Gaius, Diotrephes, and Demetrius.

Gaius is a faithful, beloved brother walking in truth, showing hospitality toward strangers, and receiving high commendation. Diotrephes is a selfish, headstrong, antagonistic, dogmatic, hateful leader in the church, seeking to lord it over others. He is condemned by John for his attitude and conduct. Demetrius with a good testimony, receives words of appreciation.

ANALYTICAL OVERVIEW

I. Introduction (1–4)
    A. The writer (1*a*)
    B. The addressee (1*b*–4)
II. The commendation of Gaius (5–8)
    A. His faithfulness (5)
    B. His hospitality (6–8)
III. The information for Gaius (9–12)
    A. Concerning Diotrephes (9–11)
    B. Concerning Demetrius (12)
IV. Conclusion (13–14)
    A. Hope (13–14*a*)
    B. Greetings (14*b*)

PRACTICAL ASPECTS

In *Pilgrim's Progress,* John Bunyan speaks of Greatheart, who assists Christian on his way to heaven.[68] Greatheart is faithful, resourceful, and powerful.

Gaius is one of these great souls, who certainly deserves the title of Greatheart, for he too is faithful, generous, magnanimous, and an encourager—big within. There is no littleness or selfishness in him, a shining example of Christian hospitality. His spiritual prosperity and walk in truth draws praise from John. Gaius, along with Greatheart, is a noble example to emulate. Will yours be a firm determination to follow in their steps?

The Christian walk, according to John, is one that must be carried out in truth. Does not this suggest the importance of the follower of Christ to match his conduct with sound doctrine—God's truth? Does your life measure up to biblical teaching?

Jude: Wear Your Armor

Jude sounds the battle cry. A fierce conflict is waged between the Lord's faithful soldiers and the devil's sneaky deceivers. It knows no letup. The Christian must wear his armor daily for protection and advancement.

There is a picture of a warrior in battle as Jude appeals to God's people to earnestly contend for the faith (3). They must have on the helmet of salvation, the breastplate of righteousness, the belt of truth, and their feet shod with the preparation of the gospel of peace. They are to take up the shield of faith with one hand and the sword of the Spirit in the other, and at the same time pray with perseverance (cf. Eph. 6:13–19).

The enemy has made his appearance with all his deceptive power, according to Jude, turning the grace of God into a license for sin and denying Jesus Christ as Lord and Master. God's people must stand up to this vicious onslaught and give the enemy no further ground. This will not be easy and at times will be costly. Christians are to always remember that God condemns sin and instructs His own as to what to do in these critical times.

Informational Material

It seems that, especially during the last third of the first century, the church is clashing with false teachers and false doctrines. Paul has alerted Christ's followers to the dangers of heresy. Now the Lord raises up Peter, John, and Jude to warn the believers again and instruct them concerning their response to these satanic perversions. Christians must remain strong in the faith because the purity of the church is threatened.

The writer of this epistle is Jude, the half-brother of Jesus Christ and the brother of James, the writer of the Epistle of James and the presiding head of the Jerusalem church.

As a writer Jude's style is concise, descriptive, and forthright. He has a love for triads (1, 2, 11, 19), suggesting that he is quite well organized in his writing. As a student of the Scriptures he makes effective use of the Old Testament characters and events.

His epistle has similarities of vocabulary, thought, and occasion to 2 Peter.

The burden of his heart as he writes is: Remember changeless truths in changing times; be aware of what is going on and live close to your Lord.

Analytical Overview

I. Introduction (1–4)
   A. The writer (1a)
   B. The addressees (1b)
   C. The salutation (2)
   D. The purpose (3–4)
II. God's condemnation of sin (5–16)

    A. Examples of divine judgment (5–7)
    B. Description of evil men (8–16)
III. God's instruction in righteousness (17–23)
    A. Divine enlightenment on the times (17–19)
    B. Divine exhortations on believer's duties (19–23)
IV. Benediction (24–25)
    A. The promise (24)
    B. The praise (25)

PRACTICAL ASPECTS

In bringing his epistle to a close, Jude lays down five important directives for his readers to carry out:

1. *Be a builder* (20a). To remain strong in the faith, we must spend time in the Word. The Bible is a faith builder. Read Matt. 4:4 and John 15:7.

2. *Be a "pray-er"* (20b). Note this significant order: The reading of the Scriptures first, then praying in the Holy Spirit, which means praying according to God's Word, submissively and sincerely. The Word gives direction and inspiration for praying.

3. *Be a keeper* (21a). You will keep yourself in the love of God by obeying Him (John 15:10). This will make you tender and sensitive, free from hardness and bitterness.

4. *Be an anticipator* (21b). You look forward to the coming of Jesus Christ with great joy. You are like a watchman on the wall scanning the horizon.

5. *Be a rescuer* (22–23). While you seek to be strong in the Lord, you reach out to others—the unsaved who are without Christ. Seek to witness to others and win them to the Savior.

These directives are followed by a word of assurance—
God will keep you and make you stand (24–25).

Revelation:
Welcome Your King

Have you ever wondered how human history will end? I am sure you have. In reading the Revelation, we are given a comprehensive view of what will happen before the end of the world and after. Revelation is not a philosopher's speculation nor a scientist's calculation; it is what God says to us in Jesus Christ concerning the end times. Therefore let us hear God out before we draw our own conclusions based on limited human opinions and knowledge.

At the beginning of the Revelation, we are promised blessing if we read, hear, and heed what it says (1:3). Many of the truths found in this book are unfamiliar to us and difficult to understand. Nevertheless, this need not discourage us or hinder us from reading it over and over again.

The Revelation helps us live in end times and be prepared for Christ's Second Coming, when He returns to earth as King of kings and Lord of lords in regal splendor (19:11–16). Get ready to welcome your King, Who will be attended by an innumerable host of angels and redeemed men and women out of every kindred, tongue, and tribe, and nation. What a day this will be!

INFORMATIONAL MATERIAL

The apostle John, author of the Gospel and three epistles, writes the Book of Revelation at the command of Christ (1:11,19) in 95–96 A.D. during the reign of Roman Emperor Domitian. At this time, the Christians are feeling the severe pressures of persecution. They need encouragement and strength to stand the storm.

Having been exiled to the island of Patmos for his faith, John receives the Revelation from his Lord and records it. He too is a fellow partaker of Christ's sufferings and knows what it means to be true to the Savior.

There is no other book in the New Testament like the Revelation, written in apocalyptic style. This kind of writing is also employed at various times during the Old Testament dispensation. It makes use of symbols, signs, color, numbers, and sound. Angels play a prominent role in carrying out the divine plan. The purpose of apocalyptic writing is to comfort, enlighten, and encourage the Lord's people in times of distress and persecution. It has to do with the future, preparing people for the uncertain days ahead.

The principal theme of Revelation points to the person and work of Jesus Christ. This book is all about Him, giving us many of His titles of honor. Other special features are songs, places, personages, and climactic culminations.

A good grasp of the Old Testament, especially the Books of Isaiah, Daniel, Ezekiel, and Zechariah, is also indispensable. Moreover, reviewing New Testament truths of eschatology—specifically the words of Jesus (Matt. 24–25; Mark 13; Luke 21); those of Paul (1 Cor. 15; 1 Thess. 4–5; 2 Thess. 1–3); Peter (2 Pet. 1–3); and Jude—are helpful in the study of Revelation.

If Revelation was a blessing to those first-century Christians (and it was), it will also be a great blessing to God's people of the twentieth century and beyond.

ANALYTICAL OVERVIEW

I. Prologue (1:1–8)
    A. Superscription (1:1–3)
    B. Salutation (1:4–8)
II. The words of Christ (1:9–3:22)
    A. To John (1:9–20)
    B. To the seven churches (2:1–3:22)
III. The worship of Christ (4:1–5:14)
    A. Before the throne of God (4:1–11)
    B. By all created beings (5:1–14)
IV. The works of Christ (6:1–20:15)
    A. Unveils the future (6:1–17)
    B. Seals 144,000 (7:1–8)
    C. Receives His own out of great tribulation (7:9–17)
    D. Destroys natural resources (8:1–13)
    E. Punishes sinful mankind (9:1–21)
    F. Confirms His Word (10:1–11)
    G. Gives witnesses to the wicked (11:1–13)
    H. Declares ultimate victory (11:14–19)
    I. Exposes Satan's strategies (12:1–13:18)
    J. Warns the wicked (14:1–20)
    K. Causes overcomers to rejoice (15:1–8)
    L. Announces God's righteous wrath through angels (16:1–21)
    M. Judges Babylon the great (17:1–18:24)
    N. Reigns as King of kings (19:1–21)

    O. Puts an end to Satan (20:1–10)

    P. Judges all mankind (20:11–15)

V. The wonders of Christ (21:1–22:5)

    A. The new heaven and the new earth (21:1–8)

    B. The new Jerusalem (21:9–27)

    C. The water of life and the tree of life (22:1–5)

VI. Epilogue (22:6–21)

    A. Christ's final words (22:6–20)

    B. Benediction (22:21)

PRACTICAL ASPECTS

Revelation, the last book of the Bible, is a fitting conclusion to all that God has said over the hundreds of years through His servants, the inspired writers. In one sense, it is a masterpiece of summary of all truth thus far revealed; in another, it is a further disclosure of what is to come.

Revelation gives us insight into the government of God, the administrator of divine justice. God is sovereign, in absolute control of His creation and the nations, ruling and overruling as He—always without exception—knows what to do, how to do it, when, where, and why it should be done, and who is to be involved in His process. His enemies will be overcome and feel His pain; His people will be blessed and feel His joy. God is on His throne forever. There will be the ultimate triumph of righteousness!

Because God is so great and good, should not this be incentive enough to turn your life—all you are and have—over to Him, letting Him be your Lord and King forever? This is one decision you will never regret and will cause you to rejoice forever.

Another Reminder

If you have been disappointed or frustrated in your Bible reading, let me encourage you to turn once again to the sacred pages of Scripture. God intends that the reading of His Word should impact your life greatly and that yours will be a satisfying experience in so doing. Don't give up! Ultimately, change is possible and you will never be the same. Therefore, continue going to His Word.

To review: *Becoming Bible-Friendly* is intended to serve as a primer for acquaintance with Scripture. It is for you who are young in the faith and for you who have read the Bible for years. It is a profitable practice to review and brush up on the content of individual biblical books. Therefore *Becoming Bible-Friendly* is written in short, concise sentences. It is easy to get a handle on, so you may gain a comprehensive view of each book read.

In reading the Bible, you will observe that it opens up a door to the past. Its history is recorded in order that you may be knowledgeable of what God has done in our world—what He did, why He did it, how He did it, what He approved, and what He condemned. Bible reading makes us God-conscious concerning the past. You will need this perspective to evaluate the present and to anticipate the future, lest you repeat the acts of wrongdoing. The Bible keeps you on track spiritually.

The Bible also broadens your horizons for the present. It is true that the Christian walks on a narrow road—the way of Christ. Nevertheless, the narrow way has broad and limitless horizons with its vast expanse and variety of realities. There are heights and depths and lengths and breadths that can only be attained by knowing what God continues to say to us in His Word in our times. The Bible is for the present.

Finally, Scripture enlightens and brightens your hope for the future. God would have you know that this earthly life is not all that He intends for you to experience. He has innumerable blessings awaiting those who have trusted Jesus Christ as Lord and Savior.

This is my one last appeal: Turn to the Bible and behold the awesome God and His Christ, allowing the Holy Spirit to guide you into all truth (John 16:13–14).

May your blessings be multiplied!

Endnotes

1   Gwynn M. Day, *The Wonder of the Word* (Westwood, N.J.: Fleming H. Revell, 1947), 19; quoted in Clarence Flynn, *Deathless Truth*.

2   David O. Fuller, ed., *Valiant for Truth* (Philadelphia: J. B. Lippincott Co., 1961), 155.

3   G. Campbell Morgan, *Living Messages of the Books of the Bible: Genesis–Malachi,* 2 vols. (New York: Fleming H. Revell, 1912), 1:16–17.

4   Ibid., 29, 31, 32.

5   Gleason L. Archer Jr., *Old Testament Introduction* (Chicago: Moody Press, 1964), 228.

6   Oswald T. Allen, "Leviticus" in *The New Bible Commentary,* ed. F. Davidson (Grand Rapids: Wm. B. Eerdmans, 1953), 135.

7   Morgan, *Living Messages,* 1:57, 58, 61, 62.

8   Warren W. Wiersbe, *Real Worship* (Nashville: Oliver Nelson, 1986), 27.

9   Morgan, *Living Messages,* 66.

10 Ibid., 88.

11 G. T. Manley, "Deuteronomy" in *The New Bible Commentary,* 195.

12 Morgan, *Living Messages,* 99.

13 J. B. Payne, "Judges, Book Of" in *The New Bible Dictionary,* ed. J. D. Douglas (Grand Rapids: Wm. B. Eerdmans, 1962), 679.

14 John B. Graybill, "Judges, Book Of" in *The Zondervan Pictorial Bible Dictionary,* ed. Merrill C. Tenney (Grand Rapids: Zondervan Publishing House, 1963), 459.

15 A. Macdonald, "Ruth" in *The New Bible Commentary,* 258.

16 Edward J. Young, *An Introduction to the Old Testament* (Grand Rapids: Wm. B. Eerdmans, 1949), 359.

17 Archer, *Old Testament Introduction,* 267.
18 Charles R. Erdman, *Your Bible and You* (Philadelphia: John C. Winston Co., 1950), 51.
19 Josephus, *The Works of Josephus: New Updated Edition,* trans. William Whinston (Peabody, Mass.: Hendrickson Publishers, 1987), 149.
20 C. F. Keil and F. Delitzsch, "The Book of Ruth" in *Biblical Commentary on the Old Testament,* trans. James Martin (Grand Rapids: Wm. B. Eerdmans, reprint ed., 1950), 494, citing Brentius.
21 Harold Lindsell, *Harper Study Bible,* Revised Standard Version (New York: Harper and Row, 1964), 391.
22 Morgan, *Living Messages,* 161.
23 Young, *Introduction to Old Testament,* 198–199.
24 Morgan, *Living Messages,* 163.
25 John A. Martin, "Ezra" in *The Bible Knowledge Commentary, Old Testament,* eds. John F. Walvoord and Roy B. Zuck (Wheaton: Victor Books, 1985), 652.
26 Morgan, *Living Messages,* 243.
27 J. S. Wright, "Purim" in *The New Bible Dictionary,* 1065.
28 Leslie S. M'Caw, "The Psalms" in *The New Bible Commentary,* 413.
29 W. A. Rees and Andrew F. Walls, "The Proverbs" in *The New Bible Commentary,* 517.
30 *Encyclopedia Britannica,* 1950 ed., s.v. "Lizard" by H. W. Parker.
31 *The World Book Encyclopedia,* 1961 ed., s.v. "Lizard" by Clifford H. Pope.
32 Wick Bromhall, "Ecclesiastes" in *The Zondervan Pictorial Bible Dictionary,* 231.
33 Archer, *Old Testament Introduction,* 353.
34 Morgan, *Living Messages,* 2:166–168.
35 Lindsell, *Harper Study Bible,* 1338.
36 Kyle M. Yates, *Preaching From the Prophets,* 7th ed. (Nashville: Broadman Press, 1942), 42.
37 Homer Hailey, *A Commentary on the Minor Prophets* (Grand Rapids: Baker Book House, 1972), 402.
38 Graham Scroggie, *Know Your Bible,* vol. 2 (London: Pickering & Inglis, Ltd., 1940), 38.
39 Donald Guthrie, *New Testament Introduction, The Gospels and Acts* (Chicago: InterVarsity Press, 1965), 23.

40 R. V. G. Tasker, "Matthew, Gospel Of" in *The New Bible Dictionary*, 795.

41 Everett F. Harrison, *Introduction to the New Testament* (Grand Rapids: Wm. B. Eerdmans, 1964), 163.

42 Ralph Earle, "Mark, Gospel Of" in *Zondervan Pictorial Bible Dictionary*, citing Irenaeus, 510.

43 Charles R. Erdman, *The Gospel of Mark* (Philadelphia: Westminster Press, 1945), 5, 12.

44 John H. Kerr, *Introduction to New Testament Study* (New York: Fleming H. Revell, 1931), 41.

45 Merrill C. Tenney, *New Testament Survey* (Grand Rapids: Wm. B. Eerdmans, 1961), 164.

46 J. N. Geldenhuys, "Luke, Gospel Of" in *New Bible Dictionary*, 758.

47 Kerr, *Introduction to New Testament Study*, 47.

48 John MacArthur Jr., "The Gospel of John," notebook, 1.

49 Erdman, *Your Bible and You*, 125.

50 R. C. H. Lenski, *St. John's Gospel* (Minneapolis: Augsburg Publishing House, 1961), 76.

51 E. M. Blaiklock, *The Acts of the Apostles* (Grand Rapids: Wm. B. Eerdmans, 1959), 17.

52 William S. LaSor, *Church Alive* (Glendale: Gospel Light Publications, 1972), 20.

53 F. F. Bruce, "The Acts of the Apostles" in *The New Bible Commentary*, 898, citing Sir William Ramsay.

54 Richard B. Rackham, *The Acts of the Apostles* (Grand Rapids: Baker Book House, 1964), xxxvii–xxxli.

55 Morgan, *Living Messages: The New Testament*, 1:93.

56 Farrar cited by Graham Scroggie, *Know Your Bible*, 124.

57 J. J. Lias, "The Second Epistle to the Corinthians" in *The Cambridge Bible for Schools and Colleges*, ed. J. J. S. Perowne (Cambridge: University Press, 1897), 8.

58 Dave Cook, "It May Be," publisher unknown.

59 Bishop Kennedy, commenting in *Newsweek*, March 28, 1953.

60 Donald K. Campbell, "Galatians" in *The Bible Knowledge Commentary: New Testament*, eds. John F. Walvoord and Roy B. Zuck (Wheaton: Victor Books, 1983), 587.

61 Tenney, *New Testament Survey*, 323.

62 R. C. H. Lenski, *St. Paul's Epistles to the Galatians, Ephesians, and Philippians* (Minneapolis: Augsburg Publishing House, 1961), 691.

63 Erdman, *Your Bible and You,* 145.
64 William F. Arndt and F. Wilbur Gingrich, *A Greek-English Lexicon of the New Testament,* 4th rev. ed. (Chicago: University of Chicago Press, 1957), 97.
65 Harrison, *Introduction to the New Testament,* 326.
66 Charles R. Erdman, *The Epistle to the Hebrews,* (Philadelphia: Westminster Press, 1934), 9.
67 William Barclay, *The Letters of James and Peter* (Philadelphia: Westminster Press, 1960), 197.
68 John Bunyan, *The Pilgrim's Progress* (Virginia Beach, Va.: CBN University Press, 1978), 227–300.

A Suggested Bibliography

Archer, Gleason L., Jr. *Old Testament Introduction*. Chicago: Moody Press, 1964.

Blaiklock, E. M. *Cities of the New Testament*. Westwood, N.J.: Fleming H. Revell, 1965.

Briscoe, D. Stuart. *Spirit Life*. Old Tappan, N.J.: Fleming H. Revell, 1983.

Carcopino, Jerome. *Daily Life in Ancient Rome*. Edited by Henry T. Rowell. Translated by E. O. Lorimer. New Haven: Yale University Press, 1940.

Chafer, Lewis Sperry. *He That Is Spiritual*. Grand Rapids: Zondervan Publishing House, 1967.

Colson, Charles. *Loving God*. Grand Rapids: Zondervan Publishing House, 1983.

Daniel-Rops, Henri. *Daily Life in the Time of Jesus*. Translated by Patrick O'Brian. New York: Hawthorn Books, 1962.

Day, Gwynn M. *The Wonder of the Word*. Westwood, N.J.: Fleming H. Revell, 1947.

Dobson, James. *When God Doesn't Make Sense*. Wheaton: Tyndale House Publishers, 1993.

Douglas, D. J., ed. *The New Bible Dictionary*. Grand Rapids: Wm. B. Eerdmans Publishing Co., 1962.

Erdman, Charles R. *Your Bible and You.* Philadelphia: John C. Winston Co., 1950.

Evans, Colleen Townsend. *A Deeper Joy.* Old Tappan, N.J.: Fleming H. Revell, 1982.

Evans, William. *The Book of Books.* Chicago: The Bible Institute Colportage Association, 1902.

Gerig, Jared F. *The Conflict—From Eden to Eternity.* Elkhart, Ind.: Bethel Publishing, 1990.

Gundry, Robert H. *A Survey of the New Testament.* Grand Rapids: Zondervan Publishing House, 1970.

Guthrie, Donald. *New Testament Introduction,* 3 vols. Chicago: InterVarsity Press, 1961–65.

Hailey, Homer. *A Commentary on the Minor Prophets.* Grand Rapids: Baker Book House, 1972.

Harrison, Everett F. *Introduction to the New Testament.* Grand Rapids: Wm. B. Eerdmans Publishing Co., 1964.

Hendricks, Howard G. and William D. Hendricks. *Living by the Book.* Chicago: Moody Press, 1991.

Henry, Carl F. H. *Carl Henry at His Best.* Portland: Multnomah Press, 1989.

———, ed. *Contemporary Evangelical Thought.* Great Neck, N.Y.: Channel Press, 1957.

———, ed. *Revelation and the Bible.* Grand Rapids: Baker Book House, 1958.

Jensen, Irving L. *Independent Bible Study.* Chicago: Moody Press, 1963.

———. *Simply Understanding the Bible.* Minneapolis: World Wide Publications, 1990.

Kaiser, Walter C., Jr. *Hard Sayings of the Old Testament.* Downers Grove, Ill.: InterVarsity Press, 1988.

———. *Have You Seen the Power of God Lately?* San Bernardino, Ca.: Here's Life Publishers, 1987.

Leigh, Ronald W. *Direct Bible Discovery.* Nashville: Broadman Press, 1982.

Lewis, C. S. *The Problem of Pain.* New York: The Macmillan Co., 1962.

Life Application Bible. Wheaton: Tyndale House Publishers, 1988.

Little, Paul. *Know What and Why You Believe.* Wheaton: Victor Books, 1980.

McDowell, Josh and Don Steward. *Answers to Tough Questions.* San Bernardino, Ca.: Here's Life Publishers, 1980.

Mears, Henrietta C. *What the Bible Is All About.* Minneapolis: World Wide Publications, 1966.

Morgan, G. Campbell. *Living Messages of the Books of the Bible: Genesis-Malachi.* New York: Fleming H. Revell, 1912.

————. *Living Messages of the Books of the Bible: Matthew-Revelation.* New York: Fleming H. Revell, 1912.

Palmer, W. Robert. *How to Understand the Bible.* Cincinnati: Standard Publishing, 1965.

Perry, Lloyd M. and Robert D. Culver. *How to Search the Scriptures.* Grand Rapids: Baker Book House, 1967.

Petersen, Eugene H. *The Message.* Colorado Springs: NavPress, 1993.

Pfeiffer, Charles F., ed. *The Biblical World.* Grand Rapids: Baker Book House, 1966.

Ramm, Bernard L. and others. *Hermeneutics.* Grand Rapids: Baker Book House, 1967.

Ridderbos, H. N. *The Authority of the New Testament Scriptures.* Translated by H. De JonGate. Philadelphia: Presbyterian and Reformed Publishing Co., 1963.

Rinehart, Stacy and Paula. *Living in Light of Eternity.* Colorado Springs: NavPress, 6.

Schaeffer, Francis A. *The Great Evangelical Disaster.* Westchester, Ill.: Crossway Books, 1984.

Schultz, Samuel J. *The Old Testament Speaks*. New York: Harper & Row Publishers, 1960.

————. *The Prophets Speak*. New York: Harper and Row Publishers, 1968.

Smith, Wilbur M. *A Treasury of Books for Bible Study*. Natick, Ma.: W. A. Wilde Co., 1960.

Spiritual Counseling Department. *The Billy Graham Christian Worker's Handbook*. Minneapolis: World Wide Publications, 1984.

Sproul, R. C. *Knowing Scripture*. Downers Grove: Inter-Varsity Press, 1977.

Stott, John R. W. *Understanding the Bible*. Glendale: Gospel Light Publications, 1972.

Tan, Paul Lee. *Literal Interpretation of the Bible*. Rockville, Md.: Assurance Publishers, 1978.

Tenney, Merrill C. *New Testament Survey*. Grand Rapids: Wm. B. Eerdmans Publishing Co., 1961.

————. *New Testament Times*. Grand Rapids: Wm. B. Eerdmans Publishing Co., 1965.

————, ed. *The Zondervan Pictorial Bible Dictionary*. Grand Rapids: Zondervan Publishing House, 1967.

Torrey, R. A. *Getting Gold Out of the Word of God*. New York: Fleming H. Revell, 1925.

Wald, Oletta. *The Joy of Discovery*. Minneapolis: Bible Banner Press, 1956.

Walvoord, John F., ed. *Inspiration and Interpretation*. Grand Rapids: Wm. B. Eerdmans Publishing Co., 1957.

To order additional copies of:

Becoming Bible-Friendly

send $12.99 plus $3.95 shipping and handling to:

Books, Etc.
PO Box 1406
Mukilteo, WA 98275

or have your credit card ready and call:

(800) 917-BOOK